THE HERMITAGE, LENINGRAD:
GOTHIC & RENAISSANCE TAPESTRIES

THE HERMITAGE, LENINGRAD:
GOTHIC & RENAISSANCE TAPESTRIES

TEXT AND NOTES BY N. Y. BIRYUKOVA

PHOTOGRAPHY BY W. AND B. FORMAN

PAUL HAMLYN • LONDON

Photography by W. and B. Forman
Graphic design by B. Forman
Translated by Philippa Hentgès
Joint production of Artia, Prague
and Sovetsky Khudozhnik, Leningrad
for Paul Hamlyn
Drury House • Russell Street • London
© Artia, Prague, 1965
Printed in Czechoslovakia by Svoboda
S 1725

LIST OF CONTENTS

The collection of tapestries in the Hermitage Museum, Leningrad, is the finest in the Soviet Union, covering, with its three hundred pieces, the main stages of development of tapestry weaving over the centuries. There are rare hangings from Germany, France and Flanders dating from the fifteenth century and the beginning of the sixteenth, as well as some Italian and Flemish master-pieces from the middle and latter half of the sixteenth century. However, the bulk of the collection is made up of Flemish and French tapestries of the seven-teenth and eighteenth centuries.[1] There are also a few fine specimens of English and Spanish tapestry of the same period, and many French, Belgian, English and German pieces representing nineteenth-century tapestry from western Europe.

The Hermitage collection as it is today was assembled after the Socialist Revolution of 1917. Its importance lies in the fact that it includes the tapestries that had belonged to the Russian tsars and also others that had been acquired by private collectors in the course of two hundred years, during the eighteenth, nineteenth and early twentieth centuries. The Hermitage collection is growing all the time and during the last twenty years some sixty pieces have been added to it, dating from the sixteenth, seventeenth and eighteenth centuries.

As early as the seventeenth century, there was a certain number of tapestries in the state of Muscovy. In 1668, Tsar Alexei Mikhailovich sent a mission to Philip IV of Spain and to Louis XIV of France. On September 13, the tsar's steward, Peter Potemkin, who led the mission, visited the Gobelins factory with his son Stephen and the clerk Simeon. They were accompanied by Charles Lebrun himself, and were given fourteen tapestries as a present from the king.[2]

In 1673, a Swedish mission visited Moscow. One of its members, Captain Eric Palmquist, left an interesting diary and some reliable sketches of his visit. One of the drawings shows the Swedish ambassador being received by Tsar Alexei Mikhailovich, in the throne room. The rich hangings on the walls are decorated with elaborate many-figured compositions.[3]

Tapestries also hung in the homes of certain Moscow boyars and princes such as V. V. Golitsyn,[4] but in general, at that time, the palaces of the tsar and the

---

[1] Gobelins *is the name commonly given on the continent of Europe (but not in English) to tapestry woven in the state factory in Paris which was first opened in the seventeenth century on the premises of an old dye-works belonging to the Gobelin family. This name was given first to the factory and then to the hangings woven in it. Sometimes the name is also used as a synonym for 'tapestry' generally, but this is not strictly correct.*

[2] M. Fenaille. Etat général des Tapisseries. *Paris, 1903, vol. II, p. 23.*

[3] S. N. Shubinsky. Istoricheskie ocherki i rasskazy. *Saint Petersburg, 1893, p. 9.*

[4] N. E. Sabelin. Domashnii byt russkikh tsarei. *Moscow, 1895, vol. I, pp. 549—66.*

houses of the boyars were seldom decorated with tapestry, and those hangings that may have existed have not come down to us.

It was not until the eighteenth century that the Russian court and nobility began to acquire a large number of Flemish and French tapestries. This is why the hangings that adorned the tsar's residence and the palaces of the great aristocrats date, for the most part, from the eighteenth century and why there are none earlier than the middle of the seventeenth century. Mediaeval and Renaissance tapestries had gone out of fashion and remained forgotten. When towards the end of the nineteenth century interest in them revived, Russian antiquarians and collectors began to acquire them at auctions and sales. It was then that the first sixteenth-century tapestries came to the Hermitage.

In 1885-6 the museum bought the collection of the great connoisseur of mediaeval and Renaissance art, A. P. Basilevsky. This collection included two outstanding tapestries from the series entitled The Story of the Virgin Mary. They were probably woven in France at the beginning of the sixteenth century. Two other tapestries from the same series were bought by the Hermitage Museum from Prince G. G. Gagarin in 1887. For many years these were the only early tapestries in the museum. After the Revolution, however, more mediaeval tapestries were discovered and the collection belonging to the Museum of the School of Applied Arts, founded in St Petersburg by A. L. Stieglitz, was handed over to the Hermitage. The Applied Arts Museum had built up its collection mainly at the end of the nineteenth century and during the first few years of the twentieth, with fine examples of western European work bought at auctions in Vienna and Paris. Among these were the magnificent early sixteenth-century tapestries belonging to various Brussels series, such as The Romaunt of the Rose, The Story of the Swan Knight, The Story of Mestra, and The Legend of Our Lady of the Sablon, which came from the famous Spitzer and Wallace collections. There were also several pieces on allegorical and mythological themes, interesting German fragments of the fifteenth and sixteenth centuries and French tapestries from the end of the fifteenth and early sixteenth centuries.

Today there are over twenty tapestries in the Hermitage dating from the fifteenth and early sixteenth centuries. They are particularly interesting because they are, in a number of cases, unique works of great artistic value. Some of them have not been published before, and, since they are practically unknown outside the U.S.S.R., have not been included in the works of most western European writers on tapestry. Apart from mentioning the fact that one of the four scenes from The Legend of Our Lady of the Sablon is in the Hermitage, monographs on tapestry ignore the Hermitage collection. That is why we have set out to inform the public of the Hermitage collection of western European tapestry from the fifteenth century to the early sixteenth century.

Tapestry is the name given to wall-hangings woven in a special way, with scenes or ornamental designs. The technique of tapestry weaving entails much difficult work. Besides great manual skill, the tapestry weaver must also have a good knowledge of design and a fine feeling for colour.

The model copied by the weaver is called a *cartoon*. The maker of the cartoon takes the original sketch of the artist and enlarges it to the exact size the tapestry is to be. He uses special materials to paint his cartoon, either colour washes on thick paper or oils on canvas. In the Middle Ages, illuminations from manuscripts were often taken as models; later, in the eighteenth and nineteenth centuries, oil paintings were used.

When the weaver reproduced the cartoon in his wools and silks, he usually made his own choice of colour and would even make changes in the details of the composition. But in the eighteenth and nineteenth centuries, tapestry weaving fell more and more under the influence of easel painting and tapestries became little more than woven pictures.

The result was that tapestry lost its own specific qualities, which had been determined by the medium and its practical purpose; that is, it lost its monumental pictorial character, its characteristic decorative effects, the flat, unrelieved treatment of the subject, and simple, bold use of colour. The tapestry designer of a later period insisted on an exact copy of the original picture, nothing less; he forbade the weaver to take any initiative, reducing him to the role of a mere copyist.

The weaver's task is to interpret the cartoon. He weaves the coloured threads of the weft into the warp, covering with colour just the exact space needed for that particular shade, and then pulling the loose ends through to the back, the side from which he works. The long slits between the warp threads at the edges of two different patches of colour are brought together either by interlocking adjacent wefts or by carefully sewing them together when the whole tapestry is finished. Joins which cross the warp diagonally are made by a series of horizontal 'steps' of different sizes.

When the cartoons showed a gradual change from one colour to another, the mediaeval weaver or the sixteenth-century artisan, who had only a comparatively small variety of tints to work with, used a special method of shading. The area between two neighbouring sections which were sharply contrasted, either in colour or in the depth of the shade, was filled in by long flecks or dots of both shades, which created the illusion of an intermediary tone. For example, if a red plane was joined to a white plane by long fine flecks, the result would be a rose-coloured area between them. The weaver also used shading to achieve an effect of light and shade and to give an impression of volume. This method was still fairly widely practised in the seventeenth century, but after that it went out of use in tapestry weaving.

In the eighteenth and nineteenth centuries, the desire to make an exact copy of the original led to the creation of a great variety of tints, for the weaver had to have a choice of hundreds of different colours. Until the early nineteenth century only vegetable or animal colourings were used, such as dye-woods, cochineal, indigo and other natural dyes, used in conjunction with various mordants. In the mid-nineteenth century the development of organic chemistry led to the widespread use of synthetic dyes which were at first much less durable than the old dyes. This is why the nineteenth-century tapestries have faded to a much greater extent than earlier tapestries.

Coarse, twisted strands of unbleached wool or linen were used to make the warp. Twisted strands of dyed wool or silk were used for the weft. Woollen thread, with its dull, light-absorbing surface, is particularly effective for deeper colours and darker parts. It throws into brilliant contrast the gleaming silk thread used for the brighter colours and highlights. In the nineteenth century, silk thread was often used alone; this deprived the tapestry of its contrasting colour relationships and practically destroyed the ribbed texture so characteristic of the earlier work.

In the fifteenth century, weavers used metal thread called *Cyprus gold*, made by winding fine strips of gold or silver wire about a silk or linen thread. The metal's shimmer gave the tapestry a still richer and more magnificent appearance. But the silver tarnished with time, and the original colour harmony was lost. By the eighteenth century its use had almost ended.

In 'rep' or corded weaving, the fine weft threads are pulled close together by means of a special comb so that they completely cover the few thick warp threads, on both the right and the wrong side of the tapestry. The difference in the thickness of the warp and weft gives the work its ribbed character; a tapestry may be fine or coarse, thickly corded or smooth, supple or stiff, according to the difference in thickness between the warp and weft threads.

In the Middle Ages, tapestries were usually long, narrow panels disposed horizontally, the composition taking the form of a frieze. Because it was impossible to place such a fabric lengthwise on a loom (for this would have meant an impossibly wide loom), the weaver had to begin his work from the side, working along to the far side, and not from bottom to top. He would thus weave the figures of people as if lying on their sides. This is why, in the finished work, the ribs of the warp seem to run not from top to bottom, but across the surface, from one side to another. Later, when the shape of the pieces had changed, this became the traditional way of weaving tapestry.[5]

[5] This can, perhaps, be explained by the following circumstances: when damp, any fabric shrinks lengthwise — that is, the warp shrinks. If figures are woven parallel to the warp, in time they will become much shorter and squat; the proportions will be distorted. But if they are woven across the warp, in time they will just become more slender.

12

There are two types of tapestry looms: high-warp looms, on which the warps are placed vertically, and low-warp looms, on which the warps are placed horizontally.

High-warp weaving was prevalent in France and the method is still used in the Gobelins factory. The construction of a high-warp loom is very simple. Two parallel rollers, or warp beams, are placed at the top and bottom of two vertical supports. Metal pins are placed in special slits along the rollers to tighten the ends of the warp threads, which are stretched upwards. The length of the warp depends on the size the tapestry is to be. As the work progresses, the woven fabric is wound on to the lower beam and the warp is drawn down from the top beam.

The weaver of a high-warp tapestry works with the cartoon behind him, reflected in a mirror beside him; because he works on the wrong side of the tapestry (which enables him to pull through the ends of the weft threads and secure them properly), the picture that appears on the right side of the tapestry is exactly the same as that of the cartoon. If he wants to copy the original more precisely, the weaver traces the design on the warp. Another mirror reflects the right side of the tapestry so that, by parting the threads of the warp, he can see the results of his work.

Low-warp looms were mainly used in Flanders. Today low-warp weaving is still practised in the Beauvais factory, at Aubusson and at Felletin. On these looms the warp is stretched between two horizontal rollers. The weaver makes a tracing of the cartoon which he then copies on paper. This paper pattern is placed under the warp of the future fabric, where the weaver can see it through the threads. Because the work is done from the reverse side, the finished low-warp tapestry presents a mirror version of the original cartoon.

However, there is no difference in texture between high- and low-warp weaving, and the method used can only be discovered by comparing the work with the original cartoon. If the design is exactly the same as in the cartoon, then it is a high-warp tapestry. If the design is reversed, it is a low-warp tapestry.

The invention of tapestry weaving comes down to us from ancient times. In Greece and Rome carpets and fabrics were made by this type of weaving. Many Coptic fabrics woven with pictorial or ornamental designs have been found in Egypt, dating from the first centuries A.D. The technique used was the same as for tapestry. When Egypt was invaded by the Arabs, the tradition of weaving was kept up. Moslem weavers took over from the Copts and, as the Arabs spread farther west, they brought their knowledge and skill to the Iberian peninsula. It is not unlikely that tapestry weaving first came to Europe through the artisans of Moslem Spain, when their work was sent to other countries. This would explain the name given in France and Flanders to woven hangings or coverings: *tapis sarrasinois* and *sarrasinoys-werkers*

('Saracen work'); or in Germany, on the upper Rhine: *heidnisch Werk* ('heathen work').

Tapestry was probably brought to western Europe in the eleventh and twelfth centuries. The great variety of uses to which it was put helped to develop its production in a number of countries. At that time woven hangings were popular both for their utility and decorative value, and were widely used as furnishings. Colourful panels hung in the halls and chambers of castles. They took the place of wall-paintings and proved to be a much more agreeable furnishing, effectively brightening up the gloom of the mediaeval castle. The thick woven wool panels did more than adorn the chambers — they helped to resist the cold seeping in from the stone walls. Tapestries were often hung from rings, like curtains, to divide off the great halls. They were also hung in town halls and in churches. Rich nobles took their tapestries with them when they travelled so that they could quickly decorate and warm the houses where they stayed. When generals went to war they lined their tents with tapestries. At tournaments and pageants, tapestries decorated the dais and stands erected for the onlookers. When kings or princes visited a city, and during festivities and celebrations, tapestries were hung from windows and balconies to make the streets gay.

There was great variety among the pictorial themes chosen for tapestries — which were usually made in series showing various episodes of the same subject. The artists and weavers liked to take the legends and myths of the ancients or tales of chivalry, unfolding long stories from panel to panel. Many tapestries recount the lives of the saints and incidents from the Old and New Testaments, as well as allegories. Today, we admire mediaeval tapestries for their decorative qualities, but we should not forget that for the people of the Middle Ages and later they had a special emotional significance, expressing ideas they held dear. These edifying pictures gave counsel and warning; they were both an education and an entertainment.

In the Middle Ages the main centres of tapestry weaving were in France and Flanders, but the art also flourished in Germany and Scandinavia. Indeed, the earliest wall tapestries that have survived were made in Germany and Norway. An eleventh-century tapestry that once hung in the church of St Gereon, Cologne, is considered to be the oldest German tapestry in existence. It was at some period divided into several parts, which are now in museums in France, Germany and England.[6] The tapestry clearly shows the influence of Byzantine art, and some experts believe that it was actually made in Byzantium. Three other tapestries from Halberstadt Cathedral are of much later origin, dating from the beginning of the thirteenth century. They are thought to have been made in a German religious house and to have been given to the cathedral by Bishop Conrad in about 1205. The style in which the design is woven resembles a Romanesque painting and may well have been taken from a twelfth-century illumination.

[6] Fragments of the tapestry are now in the textile museum in Lyons and in the Germanisches Nationalmuseum, Nuremberg. A very small fragment is in the Victoria and Albert Museum, London.

Tapestry weaving in Germany was not organised in an exclusive craft guild. Tapestries with religious subjects — most of them altar-hangings (*antependia*) or long narrow strips for decorating the backs of pews — were most probably woven in convents. The homes of the nobles were adorned with secular works showing romantic, mythological and historical subjects, or scenes with the so-called 'wild men', 'green men' or 'people of the woods' (personifications of the fight for man's erring soul, a prey to good and to evil). These tapestries were made either by artisans in small weaving-sheds, or by itinerant weavers. Rich families often had their own workers, who wove narrow panels for chair-backs, cushions, tablecloths and bedspreads.

The weavers usually drew the cartoons themselves, although in some cases the sketches may have been designed by professional painters; indeed, some German tapestry bears a close resemblance to contemporary frescoes. This is borne out by the fragments of a fresco found in Basle in 1951. A pair of lovers bearing the arms of the town clerk of Basle, Nicolaus Rüchs, and his wife are shown against a background of 'verdure' scattered with several 'wild men'. This fresco is now in the Basle Historical Museum. Dating from 1487, it closely resembles tapestries then made in Basle.[7]

Besides the similarity between tapestry and wall-paintings of this period, we can discern general characteristics common both to German tapestry and to the work of the graphic artists who designed models for jewellers, engravers and glaziers. The style of the Basle tapestries shows a remarkable resemblance to that of the Rhenish engravers.

German tapestries were made from wool, either imported or spun locally, the warp usually being of linen. Silks and gold thread were used sparingly. In the fifteenth and sixteenth centuries these tapestries were mostly hung in the houses of rich burghers or in churches. The great feudal lords, not content with the small tapestries made in their own country, ordered large wall-hangings from France or the Low Countries.

Plates
I—4
Three fragments in the Hermitage may serve as examples of early German tapestry. The oldest, dating from the last half of the fifteenth century, is part of a long narrow fabric known as the *Youth with a Stag*. A young man surrounded by animals stands out against a pink patterned background. Judging from the inscription on the ribbon-like scroll coiled around him, the rest of the tapestry must have shown a woman. The work is interesting because it is an example of the treatment of romantic subjects in German tapestry (the so-called *Minneteppiche*, or 'chivalrous' tapestry). It was probably made in Alsace, because it is very similar in style to the Strasbourg tapestries. This city was famous for its *Heidnischwerktücher* ('heathen-work hangings') which are mentioned in old lists of household goods and works of art. The *Youth with a Stag* is very like a tapestry in the Berne Historical Museum called *Suche nach Treue* ('The Search for Faithfulness').[8] Both works have much in common. The figures are surrounded by fancifully

[7] H. Lanz. *Gotische Bildteppiche*. Berne, 1955, p. 5, plate X.
[8] E. Mayor. *Strassburger Bildteppiche aus gotischer Zeit*. Basle, 1945, pp. 20—22, plate 9.

wreathing scrolls; the animals, wild flowers and plants that cover the background are extraordinarily expressive, despite the lack of depth and the conventional treatment.

Another Alsatian work of this kind, known as the Zorn-Böcklin tapestry, also has a chivalrous subject. It was made about 1475 for the marriage of Adam Zorn and Marta Böcklin, whose arms feature in the composition.[9] It is now in a private collection in Vienna.

Plates 5—8 The second fragment of German tapestry of the end of the fifteenth century in the Hermitage collection shows a stag hunt treated in a very conventional way. There is no correct relationship between the human figures and the animals in the foreground; the artist and the weaver have ignored the laws of perspective and relative size. Nevertheless, the bright, pure colours and the finely worked detail go to make up a very colourful and decorative picture.

This piece is also similar to the Alsatian tapestries, especially the one known as *David and Bathsheba*,[10] now in the Burrell collection in Great Britain, and to the *Wildweibchen und Einhorn* ('Wild Woman with Unicorn')[11] in the Basle Historical Museum. The conventional ornamental background of the earlier tapestry is replaced here by a landscape pictured with a wealth of detail.

Plates 9—12 The third fragment in the Hermitage is thought to have been part of a composition showing St Thomas and St Matthew, probably woven in a monastery or convent towards the end of the fifteenth century. This also resembles other work done in Basle. The portrayal of the figures, the monastery in the background, the great stars in the sky, the flowering plants springing beneath the apostles' feet and the range of colours are strongly reminiscent of the *Legend of Duke Henry of Brunswick* in the Basle Historical Museum. There is a particularly striking resemblance to the scene of the Duke's farewell. This fragment also has much in common with another work in Basle called the Klingenthal tapestry, which dates from about 1480, showing scenes from Christ's entry into Jerusalem and a *Noli me tangere*. This likeness is to be seen in the figures of Christ and St Thomas and St Matthew; the kneeling nun in the foreground (Anastasia Shenkind, Mother Superior of the Dominican convent at Klingenthal) is very like the nun in the Hermitage tapestry.[12]

The variations in size and the lack of depth in the treatment of figures (they are sharply outlined, their clothes hanging in deep folds), the background made up of decorative heraldic motifs and sprays of naively worked flowers and berries, the inscription on the curved scroll — all these elements

[9] E. Mayor. *Op. cit.*, pp. 22, 23, plate 10.
[10] H. Göbel. *Wandteppiche. Die germanischen und slawischen Länder*. Berlin, 1933, pp. 100, 101, plate 77.
E. Mayor. *Op. cit.*, pp. 23, 24, plate 11.
[11] H. Göbel. *Op. cit.*, p. 99, plate 73.
E. Mayor. *Op. cit.*, pp. 26, 27, colour plate.
[12] H. Lanz. *Op. cit.*, plates VIII, XII.

are characteristic of German tapestry of the fifteenth and sixteenth centuries. Despite the brightness of the tints and the contrasting tones, the use of colour is simple and, at a cursory glance, seems primitive. However, the German tapestry masters showed a fine decorative sense, a magnificent feeling for texture and a sure understanding of the medium, so that their works are among the best of this period.

Tapestry weaving probably spread to Scandinavia about the same time as it sprang up in Germany. Fragments of woven hangings dating from about 1200 were discovered in Baldishol, in Norway, with figures disposed in round arches, personifying April and May (Oslo Applied Arts Museum).[13]

No such early works are to be found in France and the Netherlands, but this does not mean that there were none. Documents of the eleventh and twelfth centuries, old chronicles and inventories of household and church goods frequently mention coloured wall-hangings, curtains and bench covers in castles and cathedrals. But it is difficult to say whether they were woven as tapestry or were merely embroidered or patterned cloth.

Early in the Middle Ages, up to the twelfth century, the monasteries were the main centres of artistic crafts. By the thirteenth century various trades had become concentrated in the towns and weaving was then a recognised craft.

The first reliable reference to French tapestry is to be found in the *Book of Crafts*, drawn up in 1263 by the provost of Paris, Etienne Boileau. French documents of the beginning of the fourteenth century give us certain indications that tapestry was commonly made and that a weavers' guild existed. At this time the main tapestry centre was in Paris. There are very few examples of French tapestry before 1400, but old documents refer to a wide range of various hangings. In the first half of the fourteenth century, fabrics were woven with coats of arms and ornamental motifs, but later birds and small animals began to appear on the cloth. After 1360 the whole character of tapestry changed; inventories from this period include whole series of woven panels with stories from the Old and New Testaments, historical episodes or scenes from poems and tales. The French kings and nobles collected tapestries, and there exist documents with the names of the weavers and bills for the pieces they produced.

The earliest French tapestry series in existence is the *Angers Apocalypse*. Louis I, Duke of Anjou (the brother of Charles V), ordered it about the year 1375 from the Paris weaver and merchant Nicolas Bataille. The cartoons for the set were drawn by Charles V's court painter, a Flemish master called Jan de Bruges, who had settled in France. The original drawings were taken from a thirteenth-century illuminated manuscript in Charles V's library.[14] But Jan de Bruges also made use of other illuminated manuscripts of the Apocalypse from Cambrai, Metz, Brussels and Namur. When the Duke of

[13] D. Arbman. *Gobelänger och andra vävda tapeter*. Stockholm, 1950, pp. 26, 27.
D. Heinz. *Europäische Wandteppiche*. Brunswick, 1963, p. 34, plate 17.
[14] Now in the Bibliothèque nationale, Paris. MS. fr. 403.

Anjou died, the set became the property of his son, Louis II; it was later handed down to René, King of Sicily, the son of Louis II and Iolanthe of Aragon, who bequeathed it to Angers Cathedral in 1480. This almost miraculously preserved set was originally made up of seven tapestries which included 105 different subjects. Only seventy-seven have come down to us. The high artistic quality of this masterpiece shows that there was already an established tradition of tapestry weaving in Paris at that time.

In the fifteenth century the Hundred Years War and the English invasion brought about a decline in the weaving shops of Paris. The weavers themselves moved on to other regions of France and Flanders, especially to Arras, where tapestry weaving had been established since the fourteenth century.

Arras now became as well known as Paris for its large tapestries, which were in great demand in Flanders and at Avignon, and highly prized in Italy, Spain and England. The name *Arras* was often given to such tapestry in England. In Italy it was called *arazzo*. By the middle of the fifteenth century, Arras tapestries were unrivalled anywhere in the Low Countries.

The Paris weavers who settled in Arras gave fresh impetus to the city's tapestry-weaving industry. But tapestry weaving stopped altogether in Arras after Louis XI stormed the city in 1477.

French tapestry weaving developed in somewhat irregular fashion thereafter, and little of its history is known. By the end of the fifteenth century and the beginning of the sixteenth, however, the famous *millefleurs* tapestries began to appear. These masterpieces of applied art bear witness to the originality, taste and genius of the French people. The subjects — rural scenes from the lives of peasants or nobles, and allegorical or mythological themes — are shown against a blue or dark-pink background, covered with innumerable sprays of flowers.

It is not known for certain where this tapestry was made. On different *millefleurs* works the same motifs recur — the same, or nearly the same, characters and the same details of landscape. However, there is often great unevenness in the quality of the work. This seems to indicate that the *millefleurs* tapestries were made by many different craftsmen in various establishments who, nevertheless, shared their ideas and designs. It is thought that *millefleurs* weaving was done in Tours and the surrounding province of Touraine, since most of these tapestries have been found in the castles on the Loire. It has even been suggested that they were made by itinerant weavers, commissioned by the lords of Touraine. According to one theory, these tapestries were made in Tournai, which remained part of the kingdom of France until the first quarter of the sixteenth century.

Plates 13—15

The Hermitage fragment known as *Youths Throwing Grain to Doves and Roses to Swine* is an example of the *millefleurs* style. Two young men stand out against a dark-blue background covered with sprays of flowers and clumps of plants. One of them is throwing grain to doves and the other roses to swine. At the bottom are three curving scrolls with edifying inscriptions. Clearly, this is one of the allegories very popular in the Middle Ages.

Plates
16—19

There is one other *millefleurs* tapestry in the Hermitage Museum, a small but beautifully preserved altar-hanging. The centre of this tapestry is taken up with the figure of Christ on the Cross. Mary and John stand beside Him. The background is of drapery, woven to imitate brocade, and decorated with a bold pomegranate design in red and yellow. The *millefleurs* element may be seen in the two side panels, in which sprays of flowers are strewn on a dark-blue ground. Here two angels in golden robes bear the Instruments of Christ's Passion. One angel holds a scourge and a whipping-post, the other a spear and a reed with the sponge soaked in vinegar.

Similar designs exist elsewhere. In Angers Cathedral there is a tapestry dating from the beginning of the sixteenth century, showing angels bearing the Instruments of the Passion. This tapestry is similar to the Hermitage fragment in composition, although the angels are more delicately drawn. A work from the church of Notre-Dame de Nantilly, near Saumur, also has angels against a background that imitates an Italian fabric. Here the angels are almost identical to those of the Hermitage fragment, with the same proportions, the same facial type and the same treatment of the wings.[15] From all this it may be concluded that the Hermitage tapestry was made by French craftsmen at the end of the fifteenth or at the beginning of the sixteenth century.

A striking resemblance of style, and a similar flower-strewn background, is to be seen in an altar-hanging portraying the Lamentation, in the Berlin Applied Arts Museum. This is thought to have been made in Touraine.[16]

Plates
20—25

Fine tapestries were also woven in the north of France in the fifteenth century and at the beginning of the sixteenth. The *Calvary* tapestry in the Hermitage is believed to have been woven there, but it may well have been woven in Flanders. It shows Christ on the Cross. Beside Him are the crucified robbers. The three figures are surrounded by guards. In the foreground John supports Mary, and beside them is Mary Magdalene. St Longinus, shown as a soldier, plunges his spear into Christ's ribs. Trees and buildings rise under a stormy sky in the background. The subject is surrounded by a border of wild roses. The work follows the tradition of Gothic art. The composition is built up of many figures without any regard for perspective, but although they are stylised, flat and even grotesque, the figures manage to convey deep emotion.

The Musées Royaux du Cinquantenaire, in Brussels, have a *Passion* tapestry dating from the fifteenth century which is thought to have been made in France.[17] The composition of the Crucifixion, with its grotesque figures of various sizes, has much in common with the *Calvary* tapestry. However, the Hermitage tapestry is closer to the work of the Brussels weavers of the end of the fifteenth and beginning of the sixteenth centuries,

[15] J. Guiffrey. *Les tapisseries du XIIᵉ à la fin du XVIᵉ siècles.* Paris, p. 88, fig. 49, p. 91, fig. 52.
[16] H. Schmitz. *Bildteppiche.* Berlin, 1922, pp. 276—7.
[17] J. Destrée and P. van den Ven. *Tapisseries des Musées Royaux du Cinquantenaire à Bruxelles.* Brussels, 1910, p. 4.

for it has the same flat and decorative treatment, the same rich ornament of the gowns, a similar landscape and the typical border of wild roses.

Plates
26—43

The Hermitage series called *The Story of the Virgin Mary* also dates from the beginning of the sixteenth century. It is made up of four pieces which apparently comprise the whole set. The columns with grotesque ornament which divide each tapestry into several parts support a frieze which serves as the top border. Three episodes are shown in the first tapestry: the Meeting of Joachim and Anna, the Birth of Mary and the Presentation in the Temple. On the second we see the betrothal of Mary and Joseph, the Annunciation and the Visitation. The third tapestry shows the Adoration of the Magi and the Adoration of the Shepherds. The fourth portrays the Death, Burial and Coronation of the Virgin.

The first and third tapestries came to the Museum from the Basilevsky collection; the second and fourth belonged to Prince Gagarin until 1887. The Basilevsky pair were published at the end of the nineteenth century by A. Darsel; they were displayed at an exhibition of French art held in Moscow and Leningrad in 1956. In spite of this, the set is still little known, even though it is an outstanding example of tapestry from this period.[18] We do not know who designed the cartoons or where the tapestry was made, but we do know that it was worked for the Bishop of Clermont, Jacques d'Amboise, who in 1490 built the hôtel de Cluny in Paris. The Amboise family arms on the tapestry bear this out.

This series is particularly interesting as an example of the transitional period. In the composition there are elements from both the old mediaeval tradition and from the new Renaissance art.

The mediaeval element is to be seen in the Gothic treatment of the curved figures with their elongated proportions, in the broken drapery of their gowns and in the sprays of flowers so typical of French mediaeval tapestry. However, the plants do not cover the whole background; they are strewn along a narrow band in the foreground; and, being sparsely used, constitute a new element in landscape treatment. The mediaeval tradition is also present in the way each tapestry panel shows several episodes. For example, in the Temple scene, Mary is in the foreground, before the priests; and far away, through an arch, she can be seen going up the steps to the Temple.

At the same time there is a new, much less stylised treatment of landscape, and magnificent perspective is used to show interiors that are no longer Gothic but Renaissance (especially in the Annunciation scene). The delicately drawn details of everyday life bring the tapestry closer to the paintings of the Italian masters. All this makes it a fine example of Renaissance art.

Although the *Story of the Virgin Mary* set is original, it does have some points in common with other French tapestries of the end of the fifteenth

[18] A. Darsel and A. Basilevsky. *Collection Basilevsky. Catalogue raisonné.* Paris, 1874, pp. 120, 187, No. 54.
A. Darsel. *Les tapisseries décoratives du Garde-Meuble.* Paris, plates 3, 4.
Vystavka frantsuzskogo iskusstva XII—XX vv. Katalog. Moscow, 1956, p. 179.

and beginning of the sixteenth centuries. There is, for instance, a well-known series of the same name, which comes from the church of Notre-Dame de Beaune. It was woven from a cartoon by the Burgundian artist, Pierre Spicker in 1470.[19] The similarity between the two works lies in the way the tapestries are divided into separate scenes by ornamental columns, in the landscape treatment and in the style of many other details (for example, the flying angels). Although there are certain elements of Renaissance art in the Beaune tapestries, evidence of the new style is much more striking in the Hermitage series. There is another similar series in Angers Cathedral, called by the same name. Here, too, each tapestry is divided by columns, and the various episodes, such as the Visitation, are very like those of the Hermitage series. The same treatment of figures and landscape is evident.[20] Many common elements of style and composition are also to be found in the *Annunciation* tapestry in the Chicago Art Institute (formerly in the Spitzer and Ryerson collections); the tapestries are of the same shape, the interiors and much of the detail are in the same style, and similar use is made of grotesque ornament and of stylised Gothic figures with gowns draped in broken folds. As in the Hermitage work, a coat of arms is woven into the composition. This tapestry is thought to have been made at Mantua, in Italy, at the beginning of the sixteenth century.[21]

Because documentary evidence is lacking, it is difficult to determine exactly where the Hermitage *Story of the Virgin Mary* was made, especially as it has features in common with both French and Italian tapestry. Most probably, it was woven in France at the beginning of the sixteenth century, from a cartoon designed either by an Italian artist or by a French artist familiar with Italian style.

The theory that the tapestry is of French origin is borne out by the coat of arms and by details typical of northern Europe. For instance, side by side with Italian architecture, we see the pointed roofs of Gothic houses and cottages typical of northern France; and in the scene depicting the Adoration of the Shepherds, one of the latter is playing the bagpipes. There is nothing surprising about the appearance of Italian-influenced tapestry in France at that time, for French art was going through a period of great change and, under the influence of Italian artists, was assimilating the new Renaissance culture.

Tapestry was developing in Flanders at the same time. By the end of the fourteenth and the beginning of the fifteenth centuries, weaving workshops existed not only in Arras but also in Tournai, Lille, Audenarde, Ghent, Enghien, Louvain, Mechlin, Antwerp, Bruges and Brussels. Merchants were exporting the products, so that an old Flemish tapestry, though

[19] J. Guiffrey. *Op. cit.*, pp. 83, 84, fig. III.
[20] E. Planes. *La tapisserie gothique.* Paris, 1929.
[21] M. Ferrero Viale. *Arazzi italiani del cinquecento.* Milan, 1961, p.14, plate XI.
H. Göbel. *Wandteppiche. Die Romanischen Länder.* Leipzig, 1923, part II, vol. II, plate 426.
E. Müntz. *La tapisserie.* Paris, p.165.

attributed to Arras, may well have come from one of the other centres.[22]

By the middle of the fifteenth century, Tournai had reached the front rank. The names of weavers owning their own workshops there and the names of many of the sets they produced have come down to us. For example, in about 1447, a certain Pasquier Grenier set up his workshop. He produced great sets such as *The Story of Alexander the Great, The Story of Esther, The Story of the Swan Knight* and *The Woodcutters*, of which fragments have been preserved. In 1449, Robert Dary and Jean de l'Ortye worked on a cycle called *The Story of Gideon*.

During the second half of the fifteenth century, many other towns had become equally noted for their tapestry weaving, and thenceforward Flemish tapestry can no longer be attributed to Arras and Tournai alone, especially as all work produced in the southern Netherlands had a common style. At that period, the weaver himself was very largely responsible for the composition, filling in the surface of the fabric with figures and details often taken from other tapestries, and choosing his own colours.

In the last quarter of the fifteenth century, Brussels became known for its tapestry. As in all weaving centres, the corporation did much to encourage the craft, strictly enforcing the guild regulations for its protection. For instance, the finished tapestries had to undergo a thorough examination to ensure that the quality of the wool and silk thread and the dyes were of the best.

The Brussels workshops reached their full glory at the end of the fifteenth century and during the first half of the sixteenth, when there was a large number of famous craftsmen and workshop owners, such as the Geubels family, Pieter van Aelst, Pieter and Wilhelm Pannemaker, van den Hecke and many others. Their workshops produced big sets remarkable for their fine craftsmanship. The rôle of the cartoon-artist now gained in importance. The first steps were taken towards bringing tapestry closer to the latest achievements in painting. Artists as well known as Rogier van der Weyden, Hugo van der Goes and Hans Memling began to work on tapestry designs.

A new style appeared in Brussels, probably under the influence of the painter Jan van Room. In 1513, he made the original sketches for a tapestry called *The Legend of Count Herkenbald* at the request of the Confraternity of the Holy Sacrament in Louvain. Maître Philippe drew the cartoons to van Room's design, and these were copied by the Brussels weaver Léon de Smet. No other evidence of the work of van Room and Maître Philippe has survived, but certain stylistic elements of *The Legend* are also characteristic of other Brussels tapestries dating from the end of the sixteenth century.

Although it still has much in common with earlier sets, the new tapestry is basically quite different. The designs are always extraordinarily rich and

[22] The only series of Arras tapestry the origin of which can be proved by documents is *The Story of Saint Piatus and Saint Eleutherius*, from Tournai Cathedral. This series had a woven inscription — it disappeared in the seventeenth century — and the text has been preserved. It stated that the set had been made in Arras in 1402, in the workshop of Pierre Ferré, at the behest of Toussaint, Prior of the Canons of Tournai.

decorative. Subjects are portrayed in great detail and each panel contains several episodes. There is hardly any interior or landscape perspective, the figures occupying practically the whole fabric. The figures wear the courtly fashions of the period, their gowns hanging in majestically sculptured drapery. Despite a certain stylisation, the courtiers express calm and dignity, turning their heads towards each other, as though deep in leisured conversation. The admirable decorative quality of these works derives from the very clear and finely drawn ornamentation on the gowns and the drapery, and from the carefully woven plants and flowers that cover the ground. The concise style, the nobility, and the restraint of the colouring (the weaver usually employed only twenty to thirty tints) give the composition a monumentality that suits the use of the tapestry — which was to replace wall-paintings.

There was no real centre to the composition in any of these tapestries; all the space was evenly filled in with figures or motifs, and there was no impression of depth. This had the effect that when the fabrics were used as dividing curtains, the vertical folds did not distort the general picture, and although the scenic aspect suffered, the most important quality of the whole work — its decorativeness — was not diminished.

Nearly all the Brussels tapestry of this period — the end of the fifteenth and the beginning of the sixteenth centuries — has a narrow border of trailing grape vines, wild roses or daisies, woven with extraordinary skill.

The Hermitage collection includes a few Brussels tapestries which are fairly typical examples of this period. Two rather small allegorical panels called *Wisdom* and *Justice*, from the series *The Virtues*, are probably the earliest. In both panels the simple composition is the same; a figure sits on a canopied throne. In the one panel sits Wisdom, holding a book; in the other panel sits Justice, holding a sword. In each panel the throne is surrounded by standing and kneeling figures, men and women in richly draped gowns which are decorated with a delicate pomegranate motif. Latin inscriptions, such as *Humilitas*, *Minor*, *Maior* and *Timor* have been woven into the drapery of some of the figures. The border is made up of wild roses and daisies.

Both tapestries can be dated from the end of the fifteenth century. They are woven from wool and silk thread, without the use of gold. The treatment of the figures and their draped gowns (which still preserve the elements of mediaeval costume) and of the ornamentation is still lacking in depth. The composition has none of the magnificence and detail of tapestry of the early sixteenth century. Both *Wisdom* and *Justice* are very like the style of a fragment of a Flemish work made at the end of the fifteenth century (formerly in the Zeligman collection), which shows a lady arming a knight.[23]

The rest of the tapestry in the Hermitage Museum clearly belongs to the sixteenth century.

Plates
44—48

23

[23] J. Guiffrey. *Op. cit.*, fig. 69.

**Plates
49—60**

The work known as *The Wedding of Mestra* is part of a series called *The Story of Mestra*, taken from Ovid's *Metamorphoses* (Book 8, lines 740—885).

The cartoons may have been painted by Jan van Room, as the style is very similar to that of *The Legend of Count Herkenbald*, which is known to be his work. The composition follows the same scheme in both cases: a central scene occupies all the foreground, additional episodes being portrayed on the upper part and on the sides as well as in the middle ground. As in *The Legend of Count Herkenbald*, the tapestries of this series are crowded with people who seem to make up the entourage of the main characters. They are all dressed in the rich costumes of the court of Margaret of Austria, regent of the Netherlands. In both cases the action is pictured against a rather stylised architectural background, representing a combination of various Gothic and Renaissance elements. In *The Story of Mestra* series there is also an absence of perspective, but its highly decorative character is brought out by the finely drawn ornamentation on the clothes, by the pomegranate motif on the materials that decorate the architectural background, and by the delightful little flowers that cover the ground.

Two other tapestries of this series are preserved in Belgium. They were formerly in the Somzée collection and were bought by the Royal Museums in 1904. Much has been written about them,[24] and an article published in 1960 gives a very detailed analysis of their composition.[25]

The first Brussels tapestry depicts scenes from Ovid. King Erysichthon orders a grove of Ceres to be cut down. For this, the goddess condemns him to eternal hunger. (Erysichthon spent his fortune trying to satisfy his hunger, and all that was left to him was his daughter Mestra, whom he sold into slavery.) In the centre of the tapestry we see Mestra, on her knees, begging the help of Neptune who once loved her. The second tapestry shows the marriage of Mestra to Mercury's son, Autolycus.

The Hermitage tapestry represents a shortened version of the Brussels *Wedding of Mestra*. The episodes and characters in the left and central parts of the work are exactly the same. The right-hand side is missing so, in order to balance the composition, the last two figures of women have been slightly changed. For the same reason, the scene of the bride and the groom which occupies the central part of the Brussels work, has been moved to the right in the Hermitage version, and only two of the three middle-ground episodes remain. The explanatory inscription is much wider; instead of the words *Deana, Neptunus, Mestram,* which are woven into the cornice of the central portico in the Brussels tapestry, the Hermitage version bears the text: *In die dedicationis di[vi]ne Neptunus Mestram recipvit deinde eam deflorvit.* Both tapestries are bordered by interlacing sprigs of wild roses and daisies.

---

[24] *Catalogue des tapisseries faisant partie de la collection de Somzée.* Brussels, 1901, p. XIV, No. 532. *Catalogue des tapisseries composant les collections de Somzée.* Brussels, 1904, Nos. 703, 704. H. Göbel. *Wandteppiche. Die Niederlande.* Leipzig, 1923, part I, vol. I, p. 411.
[25] A. van Ypersele de Strihou. *Deux tapisseries bruxelloises de l'Histoire de Mestra.* Bulletin de l'Institut royal du patrimoine artistique. Brussels, 1960, vol. III, pp. 103—112.

Plates
67—72

Another Brussels tapestry from the beginning of the sixteenth century, which came to the Hermitage from the Stieglitz collection, was earlier thought to be part of the *Story of Mestra* series. In the centre of the composition is a kneeling woman offering a richly decorated casket to an old man with a full beard and turban. They are surrounded by courtiers. In the middle ground a group of men are in conversation under a portico with carved columns, and in the upper left-hand corner the bearded old man is kneeling before an altar.

The scene has been interpreted as Mestra making her father an offering, and the tapestry has been published as part of the *Mestra* series.[26] But this theory does not stand up to analysis. First, it should not be forgotten that when, according to the myth, Neptune bestowed on Mestra the gift of metamorphosis, she repeatedly returned to her father, after taking the form of a bird, a horse or a bull. There is no mention of her taking a gift to her father.

This departure from the story of the *Metamorphoses* could be regarded as a free interpretation by the artist who drew the cartoon, were it not for the fact that there are considerable pictorial and stylistic differences between this tapestry and the authentic *Mestra* set. In the panels in the Brussels and the Hermitage collections, there are inscriptions commenting on the subject which form an organic part of the composition of the tapestry. But the Hermitage tapestry of the woman with the casket has none.

In the tapestries of the same series the form of the characters is always the same. In the other Hermitage tapestry, the appearance of the man with turban and beard — earlier thought to be Erysichthon — does not resemble the king in the Brussels panel called *Mestra Sold into Slavery*. Apart from these two points, attention should also be given to the rather different treatment of drapery. In *The Wedding of Mestra*, the folds fall more simply, being less deep and broken. There is also a difference in the design of the flowers along the bottom of the tapestry. In *The Wedding of Mestra* each stem ends in a smooth, thick-fringed root, but on the *Casket* tapestry the roots are hardly visible. Finally, the borders are different. In the *Casket* scene, apart from the wild roses and daisies there are also vines with branches of dark-blue grapes.

Plates
61—66

A more correct judgment of the subject of the *Casket* tapestry can be made if we compare it with another remarkable piece which also came from the Stieglitz Museum.[27] In the upper left-hand corner of this work a man in a fur-trimmed mantle is sitting on a throne; beside him is a woman in a mantle of ermine. To their right are a group of men, including the man in the fur-trimmed mantle. They surround a woman wearing a gown with wide sleeves, caught in by a long girdle. In the foreground the same woman is

---

[26] K. S. Butler. *Chetyre shpalery nachala XVI veka iz sobraniya Ermitazha.* Trudy Gos. Ermitazha. Leningrad, 1956, vol. I, p. 92, figs. 1, 2.

[27] N. Biryukova. *Dve shpalery XVI veka v sobraniyi Ermitazha.* Soobshcheniya Gos. Ermitazha, XXV, pp. 20, 23.

accompanied by a winged female figure with a long flowing gown. It is thought that this is an episode from a mediaeval romance. A comparison of the *Casket* tapestry with this work shows a close stylistic resemblance. The way the clothes are draped, the colour scheme dominated by blues, blue-greens, reds and browns, as well as the treatment of the landscape in the background, show similar elements. Both tapestries are surrounded by the same type of border. Probably they both came from the same set.

In his article on the *Mestra* set, A. van Ypersele de Strihou gives a detailed analysis of the characters. He suggests that one of the figures represents Jason of the Argonauts. In the centre of the tapestry there is a young man whose short tunic shows one bare foot. According to the legend, when Jason came of age he went, shod only on one foot, to King Pelias, who had usurped his father's throne. Jason could well be one of the figures surrounding Autolycus, Mestra's bridegroom, for he too sailed in the *Argo*.

The figure of the barefooted man can also be seen, repeated twice, in the tapestry with the winged female figures. This suggests that both tapestries — which we have already seen to be very similar — belong to a series on the life of Jason. At the same time, the strong stylistic resemblance to the *Mestra* tapestries indicates that all were made in the same workshop. Perhaps the cartoons for both series were drawn by the same artist, especially as the subjects are analogous.

Plates 73—74 There is another interesting Brussels tapestry in the museum, although we do not yet know the series to which it originally belonged. A queen with an ermine mantle and a sceptre sits on a canopied throne, surrounded by richly dressed courtiers. A woman kneels at the queen's feet, showing her a man's portrait. Cupid, dressed as a page, draws his bow, and one of the ladies-in-waiting holds a pomegranate. In the foreground a small dog is gnawing a bone. The border is made up of intertwined wild roses, pansies, daisies, irises and poppies.

This is undoubtedly the moment when the queen is shown the portrait of her future husband. The conventional symbolism makes this quite clear — Cupid drawing his bow at the queen, the pomegranate standing for fertility, the dog for faithfulness. This tapestry probably comes from a set depicting a mediaeval romance. With its subject and its stylistic elements — the treatment of the figures, the types of faces — this tapestry bears a close resemblance to other works, listed in the catalogue of the Somzée collection, which also depict tales from old romances.[28] This particular one depicts a betrothal.

Since no documents have been preserved we have only the style to work on. It is difficult to say which workshops made the Brussels tapestries of this period now in the Hermitage, or, indeed, the overwhelming majority of Brussels tapestries elsewhere. The same cartoon may have been copied in several workshops and, furthermore, very similar figures are to be found in

---

[28] *Catalogue des tapisseries faisant partie de la collection de Somzée.* Brussels, 1901, p. 73, No. 524, plate XXII.

different series. Tapestries were rarely signed at the beginning of the sixteenth century. In 1528, Brussels tapestry began to carry the mark of the town (two Bs flanking the town's arms) and the weaver's mark.

Plates
75—106 The two magnificent Hermitage tapestries from the series *The Story of the Swan Knight* are undoubtedly the work of one of the best workshops of the first quarter of the sixteenth century. The first one is called *The Wedding of Beatrice and King Oriens* and the second *The Triumph of Beatrice*.[29] These tapestries are fine examples of this period, outstanding for the perfection of the work — extraordinary in tapestries of such large size — for the decorative and sumptuous quality of the composition, the beauty and delicacy of the colouring and the richness of the material woven with an abundance of gold and silver thread. The unusually fine quality of the composition and the portrayal of many of the figures suggest that the cartoons may have been drawn by Jan van Room.

The subject of the set is a mediaeval legend of which the German tale *Lohengrin* is by far the best-known version. The *Swan Knight* tapestries are based mainly on the French story known as *The Swan Knight and Godfrey de Bouillon* (the Swan Knight legend is linked with the origin of the Dukes of Bouillon).[30]

This tale had already inspired earlier masters, and a mid-fifteenth-century tapestry depicting four episodes from it hangs in St Catherine's Church, Cracow.[31] Fragments of the same set (with two episodes) are kept in the Vienna Museum für Angewandte Kunst. The set was woven in Tournai by Pasquier Grenier in 1462, for Philip the Good, Duke of Burgundy.[32]

The Hermitage tapestries illustrate events at the beginning and at the end of the legend. The first shows the marriage of King Oriens to the high-born Beatrice. A scroll over the baldaquin reads: *Rex Oriens ob amorem Beatricem ducit in uxorem*, and under this the bridal pair stand, arrayed in great splendour. A bishop is joining their hands, and they are surrounded by many courtiers who are either looking on attentively or engrossed in conversation among themselves. Musicians and onlookers crowd a balcony hung with luxurious fabrics, which are ornamented with the pomegranate motif.

The legend goes on to tell of the adventures that befell the young pair. The king went off to the wars and in his absence seven sons were born to Beatrice, each with a silver chain round his neck. Beatrice's mother-in-law, who hated her, substituted seven puppies for the seven princes, and ordered her servant to take the babies into the forest and leave them there. A hermit saved the children and took the chains off all the princes — except one. Freed of their magic necklaces, six children turned into swans. Elias alone kept his human form and grew up to become the Swan Knight. When he was 16, an angel appeared to him and told him the truth, ordering him to go

[29] The total number of tapestries in the original series is unknown.
[30] K. S. Butler. *Op. cit.*, pp. 92—104.
[31] H. Göbel. *Wandteppiche. Die Niederlande*. Leipzig, 1923, part I, book II, plate 200.
[32] D. Heinz. *Europäische Wandteppiche*. Brunswick, 1963, pp. 71—8, fig. 46.

to Lillefort and tell King Oriens the story of his birth. Elias did as he was ordered, vindicating his mother whom the king asked to return to the palace from exile.

The other tapestry portrays Beatrice's triumphal return. She is shown sitting in a carriage drawn by white horses and accompanied by horsemen and torch-bearers. The ladies of the court kneel before her, their long trains wonderfully draped over the myriads of flowers that cover the ground. Onlookers crowd the balconies and windows to welcome her.

Plates
107—116 The Hermitage contains two other tapestries that attain the same degree of art and perfection. These belong to a series of *The Romaunt of the Rose*.[33] The subject of the series was taken from the well-known allegorical poem begun by Guillaume de Lorris in 1235 and finished, forty years later, by Jean de Meung. The poem kept its popularity until the middle of the sixteenth century. About three hundred manuscript versions of it have been found and it was printed again and again after 1480. The first seven editions cannot be dated with accuracy, but seven other editions are known to have been made between 1499 and 1528. This explains the appearance of a series of tapestries with this mediaeval subject in the early sixteenth century.

Judging by the fineness of these tapestries, which are woven from wool and silk thread together with much silver and gold, and also judging by their great size, their elaborate and highly decorative composition and their treatment of detail, they must have been made in one of the best Brussels workshops.

There can be no doubt about the subject, since most of the figures bear the names of characters from *The Romaunt of the Rose*. Both tapestries have been the subject of numerous studies.[34] The poem takes the form of an allegorical dream, telling the story of the young man, Bouche d'Or and his love of the Rose. Each tapestry portrays several episodes. In unfolding the tale, the tapestries sometimes change the sequence of events in the original poem. In both cases, the composition follows the traditions of the first quarter of the sixteenth century, such as one finds them in the series *The Legend of Count Herkenbald*. But in the treatment of the figures, the poses and the faces of most of the characters, as well as in certain details of the landscape, the style is very like that of the Brussels artist Bernard van Orley.

Plates
117—118 Another Hermitage fragment worked in a very similar style shows men and women against the background of an oak tree. It is too small for the subject to be guessed, but the strongly individual faces were probably portraits. For example, a bearded man turning his face to the onlooker has the characteristic Habsburg profile.

In the first half of the fifteenth century, art in the Low Countries under-

---

[33] Only two tapestries of this series have survived and the number in the original set is not known.
[34] J. Guiffrey, E. Müntz, A. Pinchart. *Histoire générale de la tapisserie. Tapisseries flamandes*. Paris, 1885, vol. III, plates 9, 10.
A. Carbonier. *Katalog risunkov masterov frantsuzskoi, italyanskoi, brabantskoi, gollandskoi i nemetskoi shkol*. St Petersburg, 1900, p. 40, No. 751, 752.
Ermitazh. Zapadnoevropeiskie shpalery XVI—XVIII vv. Leningrad, 1956, pp. 14, 15.

went a great change, with the development of new forms of economic and political life. The characteristics of mediaeval art gave way to the new aesthetic principles of the Renaissance, and there arose a desire to express the reality of the everyday world in the most direct manner. Besides the masters whose work still largely retained the traditions of mediaeval painting, there grew up a school of painters who turned increasingly to Italian art for their inspiration.

In the fifteenth century Flemish weavers worked in Ferrara, Florence and Venice from the cartoons of Italian artists. Interest in the art of the Italian Renaissance had spread throughout Flanders by the early sixteenth century, and in many tapestries of that period we can find individual motifs showing the gradual penetration of the new style. The father of the renaissance in tapestry was Bernard van Orley (about 1488-1542), who was court painter to Margaret of Austria, regent of the Netherlands. His talent and his preference for vast, elaborate compositions, his knowledge of the work of the Italian masters, especially Raphael, helped him to find new ways of developing Flemish tapestry while not completely abandoning the old traditions.

In 1515, at the request of Pope Leo X, Raphael and his pupils painted a series of cartoons illustrating the Acts of the Apostles. The tapestries were to be hung in the Sistine Chapel. Since there were no Italian weavers capable of executing such an ambitious order, the Pope sent the cartoons to Pieter van Aelst in Brussels whom he appointed weaver to the Vatican. Bernard van Orley was asked to superintend the work.

The Raphael cartoons (which are on exhibition in the Victoria and Albert Museum in London) are very different from the work of contemporary Flemish artists. They are monumental and elaborate and bear more resemblance to Italian Renaissance frescoes than to wall-hangings. The figures are given volume, and instead of covering the whole surface they are set against a landscape with a low horizon, giving a wonderful impression of space. All they have in common with the old tapestries is the wide decorative border. The *Acts of the Apostles* series was reproduced several times in Brussels and had a decisive influence on the cartoons of the Flemish masters.

Plates 119—128 One of the first sets in which these new elements of Renaissance style appear is *The Legend of Our Lady of the Sablon (Notre-Dame du Sablon)*, woven in 1518-19 for François Thurn de Taxis, master of the imperial mail. This set was never repeated. The tapestries tell the legend of the statue of the Virgin in the Church of the Sablon, in Brussels. There are four tapestries, one of which is now in the Hermitage. The others are in Brussels.

The first tapestry shows the Virgin appearing to the pious Beatrice, and telling her to take her statue from Antwerp Cathedral and have it regilded. Beatrice is shown carrying the statue out of the cathedral and taking it to the goldsmith's.

The Hermitage tapestry is the second in the set. On the left-hand side the Virgin commands Beatrice to take the statue to Brussels. In the large centre panel, Beatrice kneels before the altar of Antwerp Cathedral, begging the sacristan to let her remove the statue. To the right we see the Virgin appearing for the third time, insisting on the fulfilment of her request.

The story is continued on the third and fourth tapestries, which, incidentally, bear the portraits of the Emperor Maximilian, Margaret of Austria, her nephew Ferdinand and her nieces Isabelle, Marie, Eleanor and Catherine, and the donor himself. The appearance of these people, who have no connection with the legend, can be explained by de Taxis's desire to honour his patron. When the need for more widespread postal services became urgent, Charles V gave François de Taxis a charter appointing him master of the post. That was in 1516 and, to honour the occasion, de Taxis ordered the set of tapestries to be made two years later. He showed his fidelity to the Emperor by including the imperial family in the tapestries.

The right-hand border of the fourth tapestry bears the following inscription: *Egregius Franciscus de Taxis pie memorie postarum magister hec fieri fecit anno 1518.*

Bernard van Orley may have been the author of the cartoons. The main elements of the work — several episodes in each tapestry; traditional mediaeval treatment of the figures, with robes falling in broken Gothic folds; inscriptions explaining the action — make it very similar to the earlier Brussels work. At the same time, there is in this series a feeling of space. The interiors are treated in perspective, the figures are more natural and expressive, and the border is decorated with the grotesques typical of the early Renaissance.

This fine series is of great value, historically and iconographically. It is also of particular interest as representing the first stage of the transition to the new principles of the Renaissance. In the later work of Bernard van Orley, and particularly in the cartoons of his pupils, the new elements that first made their appearance in the *Our Lady of the Sablon* set are taken further. The distinctive and brilliant period of mediaeval tapestry comes to an end; this ancient decorative art enters a new phase and sets out on the unfortunate course which reduces it to the imitation of painting. And although the art of tapestry weaving in western Europe advanced for nearly a century and a half through periods of eminence to great artistic heights, producing many masterpieces, by the end of the eighteenth century it had largely declined, gradually losing the intrinsic qualities of the medium: the originality and the pure and logical expression which were the glory of the mediaeval masters.

BIBLIOGRAPHY

P. Ackermann: *B. van Orley as tapestry designer.* 'Art in America', 13, 1925.

D. Arbman: *Gobelänger och andra vävda tapeter.* Stockholm, 1950.

L. Baldass: *Gotische Bildteppiche aus Frankreich und Flandern.* Belvedere, IV, 1923.

L. Baldass: *Die Wiener Gobelinsammlung.* Vienna, 1920.

N. Y. Biryukova: *Dve flamandskie shpalery nachala XVI veka.* Soobshcheniya Gosu-darstvennogo Ermitazha, XXV. Leningrad, 1963. (*Two Flemish tapestries of the beginning of the 16th century.* Communications of the State Hermitage Museum.)

J. Blažková: *Les tapisseries des collections tchécoslovaques.* Prague, 1957.

J. Böttiger : *Svenska Statens Samling of Väfda Tapeter.* Stockholm, 1895-1898.

K. S. Butler: *Chetyre shpalery nachala XVI veka iz sobraniya Ermitazha.* Trudy Gosudarstvennogo Ermitazha. Leningrad, 1956. (*Four tapestries of the beginning of the 16th century.* Transactions of the State Hermitage Museum.)

A. Carbonier: *Katalog risunkov masterov frantsuzskoi, italyanskoi, brabantskoi, golland-skoi i nemetskoi shkol.* St Petersburg, 1900. (*Catalogue of drawings of masters of the French, Brabant, Dutch and German schools.*)

Catalogue des tapisseries faisant partie de la collection de Somzée. Brussels, 1901.

Catalogue des tapisseries composant les collections de Somzée. Brussels, 1904.

M. Chrestien: *La Chasse à la Licorne d'Anne de Bretagne au Musée des Cloîtres de New York.* 'Cahiers de la Tapisserie', 3, 1961.

A. Coulin Weibel: *A Late Gothic Tapestry.* 'Bulletin of the Detroit Institute of Arts', XXII, 8, 1943.

M. Crick-Kuntziger: *Les tapisseries de la légende de Notre-Dame du Sablon.* 'Bulletin des Musées Royaux d'Art et d'Histoire', 3rd series, No. 1, 1930.

M. Crick-Kuntziger: *A propos des tapisseries de la légende de Notre-Dame du Sablon.* 'Bulletin des Musées Royaux d'Art et d'Histoire', 3rd series, No. 2, 1930.

M. Crick-Kuntziger: *La tenture de la légende de Notre-Dame du Sablon.* Antwerp, 1942.

M. Crick-Kuntziger: *Bernard van Orley et le décor mural en tapisseries.* Bernard van Orley. Brussels, 1943.

M. Crick-Kuntziger: *Les tapisseries de l'hôtel de ville de Bruxelles.* Antwerp, 1944.

M. Crick-Kuntziger: *Un chef-d'oeuvre inconnu du maître de la 'Dame à la licorne'.* 'Revue belge d'archéologie et d'histoire de l'art', 23, 1954.

M. Crick-Kuntziger: *Musées Royaux d'Art et d'Histoire de Bruxelles. Catalogue des tapisseries.* Brussels, 1956.

A. Darsel: *Les tapisseries décoratives du Garde-Meuble.* Paris, vol. I, no date.

A. Darsel and A. Basilevsky. *Collection Basilevsky. Catalogue raisonné.* Paris, 1874.

M. Dayras: *Les tapisseries du Presbytère d'Anglard de Salers.* 'Cahiers de la Tapisserie', 3, 1961.

J. Destrée: *Maître Philippe, auteur du carton des tapisseries.* Brussels, 1904.

J. Destrée: *Tapisseries et sculptures bruxelloises à l'exposition de l'art ancien.* Brussels, 1906.

J. Destrée and P. van den Ven: *Tapisseries des Musées Royaux du Cinquantenaire à Bruxelles.* Brussels, 1910.

H. Engelstad: *Middelalderens Bildtepper i Norge.* Oslo, 1952.

Exposition rétrospective de l'art français. Paris, 1900.

M. Ferrero Viale: *Arazzi italiani del cinquecento.* Milan, 1961.

H. Göbel: *Wandteppiche. I, Die Niederlande. II, Die Romanischen Länder. III, Die germanischen und slawischen Länder.* Leipzig-Berlin, 1923-33.

J. Guiffrey: *Les tapisseries du XIIe à la fin du XVIe siècles.* Paris, no date.

J. Guiffrey, E. Müntz and A. Pinchart: *Histoire générale de la tapisserie.* 3 vols., Paris, 1880—1885.

J. Guiffrey: *La tapisserie de Gombaut et Macé.* 'Gazette des Beaux-Arts', 15, 1919.

31

D. Heinz: *Europäische Wandteppiche von den Anfängen der Bildwirkerei bis zum Ende des 16. Jahrhunderts*. Brunswick, 1963.

R. A. d'Hulst: *Flämische Bildteppiche des XIV bis XVIII Jahrhunderts*. Brussels, 1961.

G. Janneau and J. Niclausse: *Le Musée des Gobelins*. Paris, 1938.

B. Kurth: *Gotische Bildteppiche aus Frankreich und Flandern*. Munich, 1923.

B. Kurth: *Die deutschen Bildteppiche der Gotik*. Leipzig, 1923.

B. Kurth: *Die deutschen Bildteppiche des Mittelalters*. Vienna, 1926.

B. Kurth: *Mittelhochdeutsche Dichtungen auf Wirkteppichen des 15. Jahrhunderts*. Jahrbuch der Kunsthistorischen Sammlungen des Österreichischen Kaiserhauses. XXXII, 2, 1914.

H. Lanz: *Gotische Bildteppiche*. Berne, 1955.

E. Mayor: *Strassburger Bildteppiche aus gotischer Zeit*. Basle, 1945.

E. Müntz: *La tapisserie*. Paris, 1884.

E. Müntz: *Catalogue de la collection Spitzer*. Paris, I, 1890.

G. Migeon: *Les arts du tissu*. Paris, 1929.

J. Niclausse: *Tapisseries et tapis de la ville de Paris*. Paris, 1948.

E. Planes: *La tapisserie gothique*. Paris, 1929.

J. Pope-Hennessy: *The Raphael Cartoons*. London, 1950.

S. Rubinstein: *Tapestries from designs by B. van Orley*. 'Art in America', I, 1913.

F. Salet: *La tapisserie française du Moyen Âge à nos jours*. Paris, 1946.

H. Schmitz: *Bildteppiche. Geschichte der Gobelinwirkerei*. Berlin, 1922.

W. G. Thomson: *A history of tapestry from the earliest times until the present day*. London, 1930.

W. Valentiner: *A drawing by van Orley for the Crucifixion Tapestry in the Widener Collection*. 'Art in America', XIII, 1925.

A. van Ypersele de Strihou: *Deux tapisseries bruxelloises de l'Histoire de Mestre*. 'Bulletin de l'Institut Royal du patrimoine artistique', Brussels, III, 1960.

A. S. Verkhovskaya and N. Y. Biryukova: *Zapadnoevropeiskie shpalery XIV—XVII vv*. Gosudarstvennyi Ermitazh. Putevoditel po vystavke. Leningrad, 1956. (*Western European tapestry of the 15th and 16th centuries*. State Hermitage. Exhibition guide.)

P. Verlet: *L'exposition de la tapisserie française du Moyen Age à nos jours*. 'Bulletin des Musées de France', Paris, July, 1940.

P. Verlet and F. Salet: *La Dame à la Licorne*. Paris, 1960.

Vystavka frantsuzskogo iskusstva XII—XX vv. Katalog. 1956. (*Exhibition of French art from the 12th to the 20th centuries*. Catalogue.)

W. Wells: *Two tapestries in the Burrell Collection*. 'Scottish Art Review', VI, No. 3, 1957.

R. A. Weigert: *French Tapestry*, translated by D. and M. King. London, 1962.

E. H. Westfalen: *Putevoditel po I filialu (byvshii Musei Shtiglitza)*. Leningrad, 1929. (*Guide to the first annexe. Former Stieglitz Museum.*)

F. A. Yates: *The Valois Tapestries*. London, 1959.

LITERATURE
ABBREVIATIONS
USED IN NOTES
ON THE PLATES

N. Y. Biryukova

    N. Y. Biryukova. *Dve flamandskie shpalery nachala XVI veka.* Soobshcheniya Gosudarstvennogo Ermitazha, XXV. Leningrad, 1963. (*Two Flemish tapestries of the beginning of the 16th century.* Communications of the State Hermitage Museum.)

K. S. Butler

    K. S. Butler. *Chetyre shpalery nachala XVI veka iz sobraniya Ermitazha.* Trudy Gosudarstvennogo Ermitazha. Leningrad, 1956. (*Four tapestries of the beginning of the 16th century.* Transactions of the State Hermitage Museum.)

A. Carbonier

    A. Carbonier. *Katalog risunkov masterov frantsuzskoi, italyanskoi, brabantskoi, gollandskoi i nemetskoi shkol.* St Petersburg, 1900. (*Catalogue of drawings of masters of the French, Brabant, Dutch and German schools.*)

Collection Spitzer

    E. Müntz. *Catalogue de la Collection Spitzer.* Vol. I, Paris, 1890,

Collection de Somzée, 1901

    Catalogue des tapisseries faisant partie de la collection de Somzée. Brussels, 1901

Collection de Somzée, 1904

    Catalogue des tapisseries composant les collections de Somzée. Brussels, 1904

M. Crick-Kuntziger

    M. Crick-Kuntziger. *Les tapisseries de la légende de Notre-Dame du Sablon.* 'Bulletin des Musées Royaux d'Art et d'Histoire', 3rd series, No. 2, 1930

A. Darsel

    A. Darsel. *Les tapisseries décoratives du Garde-Meuble.* Paris, no date, vol. I

Darsel and Basilevsky

    A. Darsel, A. Basilevsky. *Collection Basilevsky. Catalogue raisonné.* Paris, 1874

Destrée and van den Ven

    J. Destrée et P. van den Ven. *Tapisseries des Musées Royaux du Cinquantenaire à Bruxelles.* Brussels, 1910

Ermitazh, 1956

    A. S. Verkhovskaya and N. Y. Biryukova. *Zapadnoevropeiskie shpalery XIV—XVII vv. Gosudarstvennyi Ermitazh.* Putevoditel po vystavke. Leningrad, 1956. (*Western European tapestry of the 15th and 16th centuries.* State Hermitage. Guide to the exhibition.)

Exposition rétrospective, 1900

    Exposition rétrospective de l'art français. Paris, 1900

H. Göbel, I, 1923

    H. Göbel. *Wandteppiche. Die Niederlande.* Leipzig, 1923, part I, books I and II

H. Göbel, II, 1923

    H. Göbel. *Wandteppiche und ihre Manufakturen in Frankreich, Italien, Spanien und Portugal.* Leipzig, 1923, part II, books I and II

H. Göbel, 1933
H. Göbel. *Wandteppiche. Die germanischen und slawischen Länder.* Berlin, 1933

Guiffrey, Müntz and Pinchart
J. Guiffrey, E. Müntz and A. Pinchart. *Histoire générale de la tapisserie. Tapisserie Flamande.* Paris, 1885, vol. III

J. Guiffrey
J. Guiffrey. *Les tapisseries du XIIᵉ à la fin du XVIᵉ siècles.* Paris, no date

R. A. d'Hulst
R. A. d'Hulst. *Flämische Bildteppiche des XIV bis XVIII Jahrhunderts.* Brussels, 1961

H. Lanz
H. Lanz. *Gotische Bildteppiche.* Berne, 1955

E. Mayor
E. Mayor. *Strassburger Bïldteppiche aus gotischer Zeit.* Basle, 1945

E. Müntz
E. Müntz. *La tapisserie.* Paris, no date

H. Schmitz
H. Schmitz. *Bildteppiche.* Berlin, 1922

van Ypersele
A. van Ypersele de Strihou. *Deux tapisseries bruxelloises de l'Histoire de Mestre.* Bulletin de l'Institut Royal du patrimoine artistique. Brussels, 1960, vol. III

Vystavka
Vystavka frantsuzskogo iskusstva XII—XX vv. Katalog. Moscow, 1956. (*Exhibition of French Art from the 12th to the 20th centuries.* Catalogue.)

R. A. Weigert
R. A. Weigert. *French Tapestry,* translated by D. and M. King. London, Faber and Faber, 1962

W. Wells
W. Wells. *Two tapestries in the Burrell Collection.* 'Scottish Art Review', VI, 3, 1957

E. H. Westfalen
E. H. Westfalen. *Putevoditel po I filialu* (*byvshii Musei Shtiglitza*), Leningrad, 1929. (*Guide to the first annexe. Former Stieglitz Museum.*)

ILLUSTRATIONS

Youth with a Stag (Fragment)

Germany (Alsace?).
Second half of the 15th century.
Wool and silk on a linen warp.
5—6 warp and 10—12 weft threads per cm.
0.25 × 1.06 metres.
No. T—2936.
Acquired from the Stieglitz Museum in 1926.
Purchased in Vienna in 1886.

This fragment shows a young man wearing a deep-pink cloak and red shoes with long pointed toes. Above him is a scroll with the words: *Zarte iu[n]gfrowe dugen[t]rich zu ungerr dienste von[nig] ich* ('Tender maid, full of grace, happy to serve you am I'). To the right of the youth is a stag couchant and part of a second scroll. The scroll must have surrounded the figure of the maid, which has not been preserved. The letters read: *it herum*. On the other side there is a black and white hound and a hare over which stretch the wings of a long-beaked bird. The pink background is woven in a pomegranate design to imitate material, and is typical of early German tapestry. The ground is covered with tufts of grass, wild flowers and sprays of berries.

The fragment is much damaged and faded.

Literature: Similar types of tapestry are referred to by *E. Mayor:* pp. 20-2, plate 9; pp. 22, 23, plate 10.

Youth with a Stag (Detail)

I

2

Youth with a Stag (Details)

The animals on this tapestry have heraldic characteristics which may even be symbolic. But the stylisation does not prevent the hare, the dog and the deer from being finely drawn and expressive.

At first glance, the work seems to be composed of several distinct elements, but in fact these elements are linked together with typical mediaeval artistry to form a decorative whole. This unity is enhanced by the decorative background and the flat, conventional design of grass and flowers.

3

4

STAG HUNT (Fragment)

Germany (Alsace?).
End of the 15th century.
Wool, silk and gold thread.
6—7 warp and 10—12 weft threads per cm.
0.87 × 0.77 metres.
No. T—2934.
Acquired from the Stieglitz Museum in 1923.
Purchased in Vienna in 1886.

A lady on a white horse and a young man sounding a horn are shown against a background of light-green thickets. Over them curls a scroll with the inscription: *Ellend in Freud dich wend* ('Grief, turn into happiness'). In the foreground, which is covered with clumps of red, blue and white flowers, the stag is at bay.

Literature: Similar types of tapestry are mentioned by *H. Schmitz*: plates 66, 67; *H. Göbel, 1933;* pp. 90, 101, plates 73, 77; *E. Mayor:* pp. 23, 24, plate II, pp. 26, 27, colour plate.

STAG HUNT (Detail)

In spite of the conventional desing of the young man sounding the horn, there is a wealth of careful detail. Note, for example, the clever way in which his clothes are worked. The young man's doublet, which has long and wide slashed sleeves, follows the fashion of the end of the fifteenth century or beginning of the sixteenth. The neck has a neat border and the collar opens to show a softly gathered shirt.

5

6

Stag Hunt (Details)

The stag and the hounds which are attacking him are shown realistically, but with little care for correct proportions or size. The background is made up of sprays of carefully drawn wild flowers — snowdrops, lilies of the valley, violets and pinks — which give the whole tapestry a highly decorative character.

This fragment has hardly suffered from the ravages of time. The clear, rich colours have kept their original freshness.

7

8

St THOMAS AND ST MATTHEW (Fragment)

Made in a convent near Basle.
End of the 15th century.
Wool and silk on linen warp.
5—6 warp and 9—12 weft threads per cm.
0.85 × 0.75 metres.
No. T—2937.
Acquired from the Stieglitz Museum in 1923.
Purchased in Vienna in 1886.

The apostles Thomas and Matthew are shown against a hilly landscape with a distant monastery. They have croziers in their hands and their red and blue gowns fall in folds. Before them kneels a nun, surrounded by a scroll with the inscription *Ora pro me St Thome*. The sky is decorated with large white stars and the rest of the background is filled in with ornamental motifs. A border of geometrical design is sewn on both sides and the bottom border is woven with a distorted and therefore illegible inscription.

The main tones of blue and red are rather faded.

Literature: *Ermitazh, 1956:* pp. 11, 12.

Similar tapestries are mentioned by *J. Guiffrey:* fig. 21, 23; *H. Göbel, 1933:* plates 32—b, 38—a; *H. Lanz:* plates VIII, XII.

9

ST THOMAS AND ST MATTHEW (Details)

The composition is typically mediaeval in its hierarchy: the kneeling nun is much smaller than the figures of the apostles. This may indicate that she was the donor of the tapestry, or possibly even the weaver. This is also suggested by the inscription *Ora pro me St Thome.*

There is a strong resemblance between the nun and the kneeling figure of the Mother Superior on the Klingenthal tapestry in Basle, which is dated about 1480.

A *horror vacui*, or 'fear of emptiness', seems to have driven the German masters of the fifteenth and sixteenth centuries to fill in the whole of the space on their tapestries. With a flair for decoration and an understanding of their medium, they mixed details of landscape with ornamental and heraldic motifs.

10

11

St Thomas and St Matthew (Detail of St Matthew)

The almost graphic boldness with which the face is portrayed, the dark eyes glancing aside, is typical of the German school. Despite the great economy of line, the picture of the apostle is extremely expressive and original.

YOUTHS THROWING GRAIN TO DOVES AND ROSES TO SWINE
(Fragment)

France (Touraine?).
End of the 15th or beginning of the 16th century.
Wool and silk.
4—5 warp and 10—12 weft threads per cm.
2.26 × 1.56 metres.
No. T—2926.
Acquired from the Stieglitz Museum in 1926.
Purchased in Vienna in 1886.

Two young men are shown against a dark-blue background covered with sprigs of flowers. One is throwing grain to doves and the other roses to swine. Over the first youth is the almost illegible inscription *Deliberen* [?] *mieux*, and over the second the words *Bon espoir*.

At the feet of the first youth is a scroll with the following explanatory verse:

Par semer en temps [et] en lieu
les pois par d[e]va[n]t les coullo[n]s
suis dont ien remerchie dieu
venus a mes conclusions

Je seme roses au poursiauh
aussitout bien comet prescheu
qu[an]t ne sevent par leurs mos bio
co[n]vertir obstines pecheurs.

Sowing in time and place
Grain before doves
Thus I have, and I thank God,
achieved my end.

I throw roses before swine
as do the preachers
when they cannot, by fine words,
convert obstinate sinners.

More than half of the third scroll is missing. Above it, on the left-hand side, is a man's figure, and it is possible to make out the end of a phrase: [...] *ra dieu*.

Judging from the type of inscription, this fragment must have been part of a *millefleurs* allegorical tapestry.

Literature: *Ermitazh, 1956:* p. 22. Similar tapestries are referred to in *J. Guiffrey:* plate II, fig. 51; *H. Göbel, II, 1923:* vol. II, plates 313, 316; *R. A. Weigert:* pp. 76—8.

YOUTHS THROWING GRAIN TO DOVES AND ROSES TO SWINE
(Detail)

13

14

YOUTHS THROWING GRAIN TO DOVES AND ROSES TO SWINE
(Detail)

The French *millefleurs* tapestries have an incomparable charm, and are among the most successful designs for tapestry ever devised. Their decorative qualities are enhanced by the naturalism of the animals and flowers which form the background. Innumerable sprays of flowers and plants of all kinds are most carefully drawn. Violets and daisies, pinks and bluebells, lilies of the valley and stocks, the flowers and the fruit of the strawberry — all are depicted with the simplicity and delicacy that distinguish the work of the French masters.

a dieu

ne

vir

sace

faire

Par semer en temps et lieu
les pois par deuat les coulles
fus dont ien remercie dieu
deuvis a mes contubions

THE CRUCIFIXION, WITH STANDING FIGURES OF THE VIRGIN AND ST JOHN, AND ANGELS BEARING THE INSTRUMENTS OF THE PASSION

France (Touraine?).
End of the 15th or beginning of the 16th century.
Wool and silk.
5 warp and 10—12 weft threads per cm.
0.79 × 1.25 metres.
No. T—2938.
Acquired from the Stieglitz Museum in 1923.
Purchased in Vienna in 1886.

The central part shows the Crucifixion, with the Cross standing out against red hangings that are covered with a yellow-gold pomegranate design. Mary and the apostle John stand beside it, in blue and red garments. On each side is an angel bearing the Instruments of the Passion. The whole is woven on a dark-blue background, strewn with tiny sprays of rather stylised flowers. The narrow border has a geometrical design.

Literature: Similar tapestries are described in the following works: *H. Schmitz:* fig. 140; *J. Guiffrey:* p. 88, fig. 49, p. 91, fig. 52; *Exposition rétrospective,* p. 45.

THE CRUCIFIXION (Detail)

An angel holding the spear and the sponge on the reed. The slightly inclined head with its long, light-brown hair, the cast-down eyes and pale yellow-gold gown give the figure the exalted look that is seen in the angels of the Notre-Dame de Nantilly tapestry.

16

17

THE CRUCIFIXION (Detail)

The figure of Mary, with a rather crudely portrayed but very expressive face, is woven against a background imitating brocade. This has a large pomegranate design in red and yellow, which is typical of the fifteenth century.

The deep-toned colours are unfaded.

THE CRUCIFIXION (Detail)

The head, and indeed the whole figure, of Christ on the Cross is treated differently from the more crudely drawn figures of Mary and John.

The spirituality and inspiration of the portrayal stand out in contrast to the background.

19

Calvary

France (?). Exact origin unknown.
End of the 15th or beginning of the 16th century.
Wool and silk.
6 warp and 13—14 weft threads per cm.
3.12×2.3 metres.
No. T—15613.
Acquired from the Stieglitz Museum.
Purchased in Paris in 1900 from the dealer Lowengard.

The figure of Christ on the Cross is set against a stormy sky. On each side are the crosses of the thieves, with a crowd at their feet. St Longinus, shown as a bearded horseman, thrusts his spear into Christ's side. In the foreground are the sorrowing figures of the women; Mary Magdalene clings to the Cross and the apostle John supports the Virgin. The background is a hilly landscape with trees and buildings.

The border has a design of wild roses and pansies strewn on a dark-blue background.

The tapestry is very faded and worn, and it is evident that past restorations have altered the original colours.

Literature: *Ermitazh, 1956:* p. 23.

Similar tapestries are mentioned by *Destrée and van den Ven:* plate 4.

20

CALVARY (Details)

The figures of Christ and the penitent thief express great refinement in contrast to the faces of the second thief and the soldiers.

21

22

Calvary (Detail)

This detail is of the group of soldiers round the Cross, among them St Longinus with his spear.

Despite the conventional treatment and even incorrect proportions of the design, some figures show a remarkable degree of characterisation which verges on the grotesque.

The atmosphere of grief and affliction is enhanced by the details of the landscape, seen through a forest of spears, and of the buildings and the boldly outlined trees, crowded together under the stormy sky.

CALVARY (Detail)

The unusual position and treatment of the figure of the second thief, bound to a T-shaped cross and surrounded by a crowd, is reminiscent of figures on the triptychs of early Limoges enamel.

CALVARY (Detail)

The group of grief-stricken women, with Mary and John, contrast with the menacing forest of spears and the crowd of soldiers.

The kneeling woman in a long, spreading gown which sweeps over the stony ground in stiffly broken folds, is the embodiment of deep and silent sorrow.

THE MEETING OF JOACHIM AND ANNA, THE BIRTH OF MARY AND THE PRESENTATION IN THE TEMPLE, from the series THE STORY OF THE VIRGIN MARY

France. Exact place of origin unknown.
Early 16th century.
Wool and silk.
6—7 warp and 14—16 weft threads per cm.
1.53 × 6.63 metres.
No. T—15614.
Acquired by the Hermitage from the Basilevsky collection in 1884.

The series is made up of four tapestries which were woven for Jacques d'Amboise, Bishop of Clermont. Each tapestry is divided into several parts by columns ornamented with grotesques, each part depicting a different episode.

The left-hand panel shows the meeting of Mary's parents at the city gates. Joachim is welcoming Anna, who is accompanied by two servants. To the right is a servant with a basket.

The middle panel depicts the birth of Mary. Anna is lying on a couch under a red baldaquin. Two kneeling women are bathing the new-born baby, Mary. The arms of Jacques d'Amboise are placed over the arches in the architectural background.

The right-hand panel shows the Presentation in the Temple. To the right, at the altar, Mary kneels before the priest who holds over her the tables of the Commandments, while Joachim, Anna and two women look on. In the distance, through a deep

26

27

arch, we can see a street with Mary going up the steps to the Temple. The arms of Jacques d'Amboise hang over the arch.

The narrow border is made up of stylised acanthus leaves in gold and brown.

The colouring of this tapestry is particularly intense — reds, dark and pale blues, greens and golden yellows, which have been comparatively well preserved.

Literature: *Darsel and Basilevsky:* pp. 120, 167, No. 544;

A. Darsel: plates 3, 4; *Ermitazh, 1856:* p. 23; *Vystavka:* p. 179.

THE MEETING OF JOACHIM AND ANNA (Detail)

The *Virgin Mary* tapestries are a fine example of the transitional period, containing both mediaeval and Renaissance elements.

The clear-cut figures of the servants are set against a background of typical Renaissance arches, but through them we can see the steep-roofed houses of a mediaeval city.

The young girl with high forehead and slender neck who looks out of the picture is reminiscent of Italian portraits painted at the end of the fifteenth century. The older woman is more like a figure from a Gothic wall-hanging, for the shawl that covers her bent head is draped in the deep folds characteristic of Gothic style.

THE MEETING OF JOACHIM AND ANNA (Detail)

The faces of Anna and her servant are full of tranquillity and dignity.

As in all the tapestries of this series, the landscape plays an important rôle, its treatment being very different from that of mediaeval tapestry. There is a feeling of depth and space, while the architectural motifs, typical of the Renaissance, show that the artist who drew the cartoon was familiar with Italian art of the fifteenth century.

THE BIRTH OF MARY (Detail)

All the scenes in this set contain a wealth of domestic detail, some of it bearing little relation to the subject. In the deep recess of a round arch, we see two gesticulating townswomen, deep in conversation.

THE PRESENTATION IN THE TEMPLE (Detail)

In the tradition of mediaeval tapestry, several successive episodes of the same story are depicted at once. In the background, through an arcade decorated with grotesques, there is a perspective of streets with the tiny figure of Mary going up the steps to the Temple.

31

32

T HE BETROTHAL OF MARY AND JOSEPH, THE ANNUNCIATION AND
THE VISITATION, from the series THE STORY OF THE VIRGIN MARY

France. Place of origin unknown.
Beginning of the 16th century.
Wool and silk.
6—7 warp and 14—16 weft threads per cm.
1.54×5.84 metres.
No. T—15615.
Acquired by the Hermitage from the collection of Prince Gagarin, in 1887.

The left-hand panel shows the betrothal of Mary and Joseph. Priests are joining the
hands of the betrothed couple, against a background of arcades. Behind them are
girls holding branches of palm.

The central panel shows the Annunciation. Mary is kneeling before a lectern and
behind it, on the other side, is the Archangel Gabriel. In the background is a colon-
nade with a magnificent perspective. The lectern bears the arms of Jacques d'Amboise.

The right-hand panel shows the meeting of Mary and Elizabeth. Mary is lifting up
the kneeling Elizabeth, beside whom stands Zachary. In the distance is a towered city.

The dominating colours are reds, blues, greens, pinks and golden yellows. The
colours are unfaded.

Literature: *Ermitazh, 1956:* p. 23; *Vystavka:* p. 179.

33

34

THE BETROTHAL OF MARY AND JOSEPH (Detail)

According to the apocryphal story, the priest called the unmarried men to the Temple, to choose a husband among them for Mary. Each of them had a staff, and he said that the one belonging to the man chosen would break into flower. When Joseph's staff flowered, the other young men smashed their own in anger.

THE VISITATION (Detail)

Mary and Elizabeth are shown against the outline of a city with an interesting variety of architectural forms and fine details of domestic life.

35

THE ADORATION OF THE SHEPHERDS AND OF THE MAGI, from the series THE STORY OF THE VIRGIN MARY

France. Place of origin unknown.
Early 16th century.
Wool and silk.
6—7 warp and 14—16 weft threads per cm.
1.53×3.72 metres.
No. T—15616.
Acquired by the Hermitage in 1885 from the Basilevsky collection.

The left-hand panel shows the Adoration of the Shepherds. In the distance, between small, steep-roofed houses, several shepherds listen with wonder to the angel who has appeared to them to announce the birth of Christ. A scroll bears the inscription: GLORIA IN EXCELSIS DEO.

In the foreground, Mary is bending over the baby in the crib. They are surrounded by shepherds and angels with musical instruments. One of the shepherds is on his knees, playing the bagpipes, adding his simple tune to the celestial choir.

The right-hand side shows the Adoration of the Magi. In the distance can be seen the procession of the Wise Men coming to adore Christ. In the foreground, Mary is nursing her baby. Behind her is a portico, and before her the three Wise Men, presenting their precious gifts.

The bottom part of the tapestry is decorated with bunches of flowers, among which appear the arms of Jacques d'Amboise.

Literature: *A. Darsel:* No. 3, 4; *Darsel and Basilevsky:* pp. 120, 187, No. 544; *Ermitazh, 1956:* p. 23; *Vystavka;* p. 179.

THE ADORATION OF THE SHEPHERDS (Detail)

The finely drawn face and hands of Mary, who bends over her Child, are in sharp contrast to the naive portrayal of the animals. In the same way, the finely drawn arabesques on the pilasters of the portico may be contrasted with the conventional rendering of the crude timber of the manger and the crib.

36

37

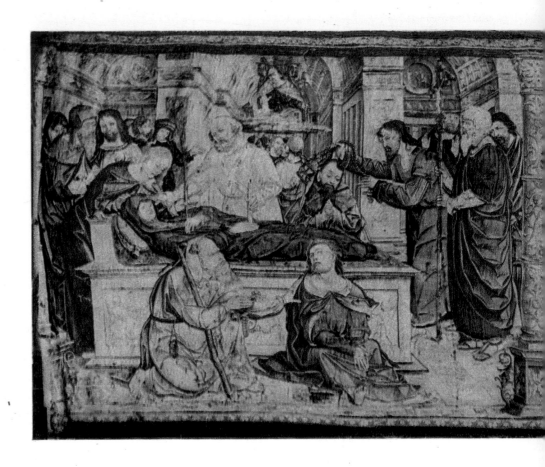

THE DEATH, THE BURIAL AND THE CORONATION OF THE VIRGIN,
from the series THE STORY OF THE VIRGIN MARY

France. Place of origin unknown.
Early 16th century.
Wool and silk.
6—7 warp and 14—16 weft threads per cm.
1.57 × 5.83 metres.
No. T—15617.
Acquired by the Hermitage in 1887 from the collection of Prince Gagarin.

The left-hand panel shows the Death of the Virgin. The body of Mary is shown on the bier. The weeping St John, bearing a branch of palm, is bending over her; the bier is surrounded by apostles and clergy. In the distance, set against the background of an arcade, Christ sits on a throne in the clouds.

The central panel shows the burial of Mary. The apostles accompany the coffin, holding a canopy over it, and on its side can be seen the hands of the profane who, according to legend, tried to prevent the burial, for which they were chastised.

The right-hand panel shows the Coronation of the Virgin in heaven. Mary is seated on a throne in the centre, being crowned by the Holy Trinity. Around them are the figures of the saved and above them angels. Some of the angels are playing musical instruments while others bear aloft a canopy with the inscription: REGINA CELI LETARE. At the bottom, among angelic musicians in flight, are the arms of Jacques d'Amboise.

38

THE DEATH OF THE VIRGIN (Detail)

The architectural background is interesting for the wealth of ornamental grotesques. The bier on which Mary lies resembles an ancient sarcophagus with decoration in bas-relief.

The expressive figures of the apostles around the bier are boldly foreshortened.

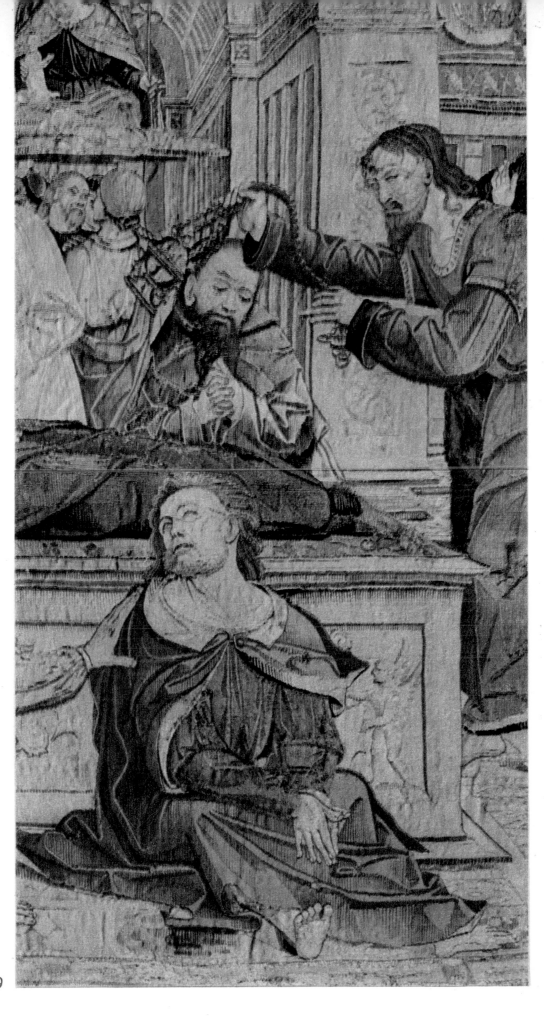

39

THE DEATH OF THE VIRGIN (Detail)

These exquisite hands in prayer heighten the drama of the scene.

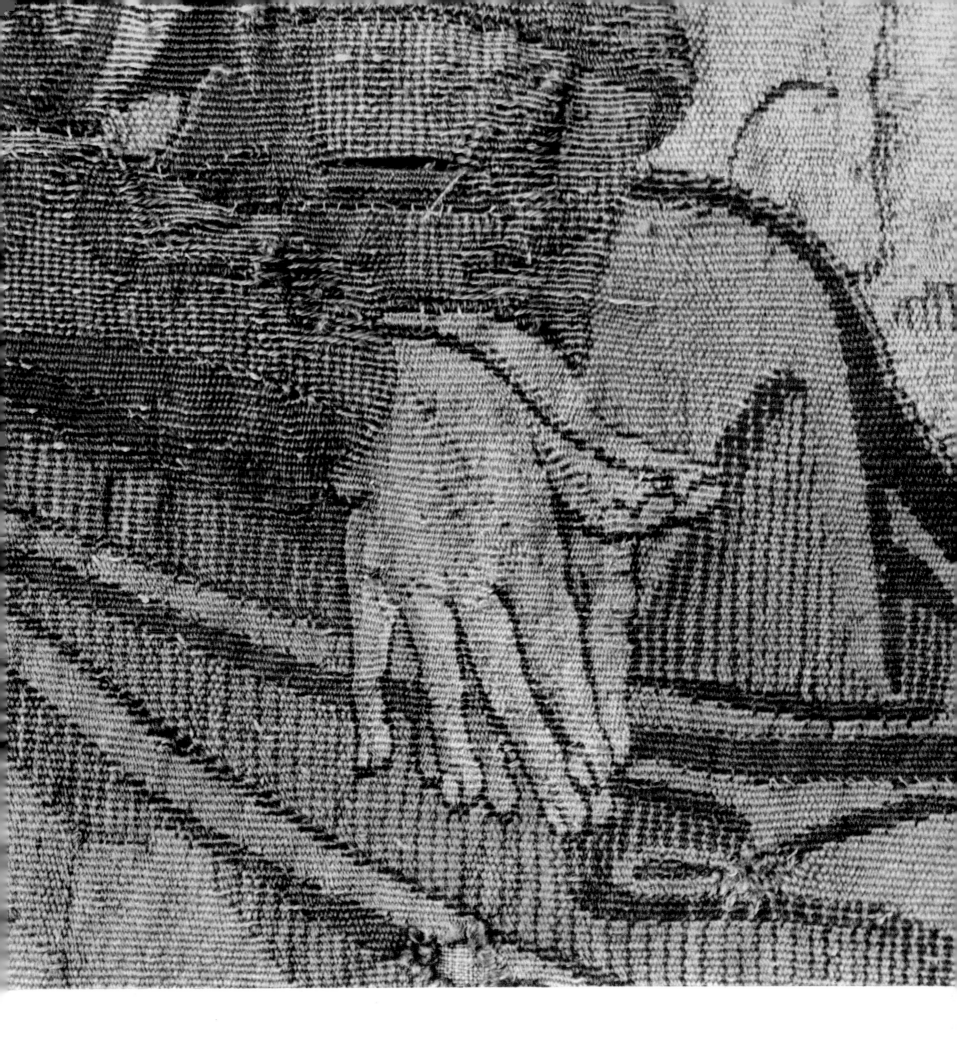

THE BURIAL (Detail)

The movement of the apostles who accompany the coffin is stressed by the contrasting rhythm of their sorrowing figures.

THE CORONATION (Details)

The treatment of the flying angels and of the angelic musicians is in the tradition of much earlier mediaeval tapestry and painting.

41

43

42

WISDOM, from the series THE VIRTUES

Flanders, Brussels.
End of the 15th century.
Wool and silk.
6—7 warp and 16—18 weft threads per cm.
2.85×2.32 metres.
No. T — 2932
Acquired by the Hermitage from the Stieglitz Museum in 1923.

Wisdom, shown as a woman in a light gown, a book on her knees, occupies the centre of the tapestry. Over her throne is a canopy with a red pomegranate design. The word *Sapiensit* is woven along the border of her gown. Around her are the figures of men and women in red and blue gowns, heavily ornamented and rather flat. The upper part of the tapestry shows a hilly landscape with a narrow band of sky. The border is made up of branches of wild rose and daisies on a dark blue ground.

Literature: *Ermitazh, 1956:* p. 14.

44

WISDOM (Detail)

The men and women around Wisdom's throne are dressed in richly decorated gowns falling in great folds. They take up almost all the surface of the tapestry. With the characteristically flat treatment of the figures, the absence of depth and space, the precise, graphic treatment of the ornamentation and, at the same time, the very expressive faces, this tapestry is typical of Brussels work in the late fifteenth and early sixteenth centuries.

45

JUSTICE, from the series THE VIRTUES

Flanders, Brussels.
End of the 15th century.
Wool and silk.
6—7 warp and 14—16 weft threads per cm.
3.12×2.45 metres.
No. T—2933.
Acquired by the Hermitage from the Stieglitz Museum in 1923.

Justice, shown as a youth holding a sword, is pictured on a throne, under a canopy decorated with blue pomegranates. He is surrounded by men and women in rich clothes decorated with red, blue and gold. Some of the figures bear inscriptions, such as *Humilitas, Maior, Minor, Timor*. These figures cover almost the whole of the tapestry, but above them there is a landscape with a narrow band of sky.

The border is made up of wild roses and daisies on a dark-blue ground.

Literature: *Ermitazh, 1956:* p. 14.

JUSTICE (Detail)

Tranquillity and wisdom are reflected in the face of the old man who leans on a long staff, as though he were listening attentively to the words of the youth beside him. The artist has cleverly filled the tapestry with people, thus enriching and enlarging a theme that might originally have been too slight on its own.

46

47

Justice (Detail)

One of the group of figures around Justice is a man dressed in a luxurious gown. A splendid cloak is flung over one shoulder. His whole appearance — the line of his face, the inclination of his head, the gesture of his hand — typifies doubt. Although this figure has no explanatory inscription, the expressive quality of the portrayal and the presence of certain attributes make it possible, in this and many other cases, to guess the intention of the Flemish tapestry artist of this period.

THE WEDDING OF MESTRA, from the series THE STORY OF MESTRA

Flanders, Brussels.
Early 16th century.
The cartoons may have been designed by Jan van Room.
Wool and silk.
6—8 warp and 10—12 weft threads per cm.
3.45×3.95 metres.
No. T—15620.
Acquired by the Hermitage from the Stieglitz Museum in 1923.

The subject comes from Ovid's *Metamorphoses* (Book 8, lines 740—885). A king of Thessaly, Erysichthon, offended Ceres, who condemned him to the torture of eternal hunger. He spent all his wealth trying to assuage his craving, and was finally obliged to sell his daughter Mestra into slavery. But Neptune had bestowed on her the gift of metamorphosis. Her father sold her many times over and each time she came back to him, having taken the shape of a fisherman, a bird, a bull or a doe. After Erysichthon's death, Mestra married Autolycus, son of Mercury.

The tapestry shows the marriage of Mestra, with a splendid bridal procession. Mestra and Autolycus are surrounded by a large suite. In the left background we see Mestra kneeling before Neptune to thank him for his gift. To the right is a tribune gaily decorated with ornamented hangings, full of richly dressed spectators. Over the tribune is the inscription: *in die dedicationis di[vi]ne Neptunus Mestram recipvit deinde eam deflorvit.*

The narrow border is made up of thickly interlaced sprigs of wild roses and daisies on a blue ground. The whole tapestry is woven in still unfaded deep blues, reds and greens.

Literature: *Collection de Somzée, 1901:* p. XIV, Nos. 531, 532; *Collection de Somzée, 1904:* Nos. 703, 704; *H. Göbel, I, 1923:* vol. I, pp. 137, 411; vol. II, plate 102; *Ermitazh, 1956:* p. 11; *K. S. Butler:* pp. 92—103, fig. 1—4; *van Ypersele:* pp. 103—12; *N. Y. Biryukova:* pp. 20—3.

THE WEDDING OF MESTRA (Detail)

One of the girls has taken a young man by the shoulders. Several experts believe him to be Jason, the captain of the Argonauts, of whom Autolycus, the bridegroom of Mestra, was one.

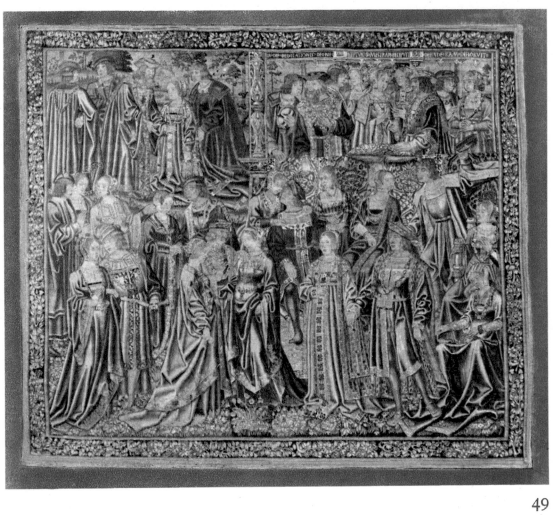

49

50

THE WEDDING OF MESTRA (Detail)

The woman with the sad face, who is shown against a draped background with a pomegranate design, may be interpreted as the abandoned Medea. She is trying of retain Jason, who has turned away from her to his new bride, Glauce, the king to Corinth's daughter, who has her arm round his shoulder.

THE WEDDING OF MESTRA (Details)

The chief guests, the inhabitants of Olympus, are gathered on the high tribune, which is draped with ornamented hangings. Among them is Venus, the goddess of love, wearing a splendid chaplet. With her are Mercury, Autolycus' father and Neptune. The sea god, who was once in love with Mestra, is shown as an old man with a full beard.

NE · NEPTVNVS · MESTRAM · RECIPVIT · DEEINDE · EAM · DEFLORVIT

52

53

THE WEDDING OF MESTRA (Details)

The bride and bridegroom are surrounded by a crowd of men and women, some animated and full of movement, others calm and dignified.

54

55

THE WEDDING OF MESTRA (Detail of a young girl and her suitor)

This charming girl stands out for the nobility and restrained lyricism of her portrayal
Looking dreamily into the distance, she is listening to the words of a young man who
is bending towards her.

56

THE WEDDING OF MESTRA (Detail)

Whatever the subject, the ladies and gentlemen in sixteenth-century Flemish tapestry always wear the costumes of the court of Margaret of Austria, regent of the Netherlands. The rich gowns are draped in sculptured folds, the long trains flowing over the ground, which is strewn with clumps of daffodils, daisies and violets. The rhythm of the drapery, the detailed and finely drawn ornament on the gowns and the conventional style of the carefully pictured flowers and plants are the elements that give Brussels tapestry its highly decorative quality, which is the essence of the medium.

THE WEDDING OF MESTRA (Detail)

The distinctive features of many of the people in this tapestry lead one to think that some of them must be portraits of the artist's contemporaries.

THE WEDDING OF MESTRA (Detail)

Autolycus, the son of Mercury, and bridegroom of Mestra.

THE WEDDING OF MESTRA (Detail)

The sensitive portrayal of the human hand is a characteristic of early sixteenth-century Brussels tapestry.

MEDEA AIDING THE ARGONAUTS, from the series THE STORY OF JASON

Flanders, Brussels.
Early 16th century.
Wool and silk.
6—7 warp and 10—12 weft threads per cm.
3.46 × 3.32 metres.
No. T—2976.
Acquired by the Hermitage from the Stieglitz Museum in 1923.

The subject is taken from Ovid's *Metamorphoses* (Book 12, lines 1—359). Aeson, King of Iolchos, had been banished by his half-brother Pelias when he usurped the throne. When Aeson's son Jason came of age and demanded his rights, Pelias sent him to seek the Golden Fleece in Colchis, where King Aeëtes ruled. Jason summoned all the heroes of Greece and set out in the ship Argo. Aeëtes' daughter, Medea, a sorceress and priestess of Hecate, fell in love with Jason, helped him to find the Golden Fleece and fled with him from Colchis. After many vicissitudes, Jason and Medea came to Corinth. But when Jason decided to repudiate her and marry the daughter of Creon, the Corinthian king, Medea sent the bride a gown and crown which mortally poisoned her the moment she put them on.

In the upper left of the tapestry Jason is vowing eternal fidelity to Medea; in the upper right, Medea, surrounded by the Argonauts, promises to help Jason obtain the Golden Fleece. In the foreground Hecate is shown as a winged goddess and Medea, her priestess, is asking her help in accomplishing her plan. The narrow border is made up of wild roses, daisies and grapes, on a dark-blue ground. The tapestry has been well preserved and the colour scheme of blue-greens and reddish browns is very fresh.

Literature: *N. Y. Biryukova:* pp. 20—3.

61

Medea Aiding the Argonauts (Detail)

Jason gives the sorceress Medea his vow of eternal love. All subjects — religious, historical or mythological — in Brussels tapestry of the end of the fifteenth century and beginning of the sixteenth, are treated in the style of contemporary scenes of chivalry.

Medea Aiding the Argonauts (Detail)

Costume detail is very important in early sixteenth-century Flemish tapestry. Much attention is given to head-dress, jewellery, heavy chains and necklaces. Some characters often appear several times in the same costume. Medea, for example, is twice shown in the same gown.

MEDEA AIDING THE ARGONAUTS (Details)

Medea promises Jason and the Argonauts that she will help them to obtain the Golden Fleece, and keeps her promise with the aid of Hecate.

The sixteenth-century artist drew Hecate as an old woman with wings. Her expressive face and dynamic movement make her a sinister figure. This witch-like portrayal has nothing whatsoever in common with the three-headed Greek goddess of the underworld; but it is how the late Middle Ages saw her.

64

65

MEDEA AIDING THE ARGONAUTS (Detail)

The remarkably expressive portrayal of the bearded man with his stern and noble face, and of the calm, pensive woman, is in striking contrast to the dramatic interpretation of Medea and Hecate.

MEDEA BEARING GIFTS TO CREON, from the series THE STORY OF JASON

Flanders, Brussels.
Early 16th century.
Wool and silk.
6—8 warp and 10—12 weft threads per cm.
3.35 × 3.42 metres.
No. T—15625.
Acquired by the Hermitage from the Stieglitz Museum in 1923.

In the centre of the tapestry, Medea presents the casket with the poisoned gifts to Creon, the king of Corinth, and his daughter. Around them crowds a large entourage of courtiers. On the left-hand side, in the distance, we see Creon kneeling before an altar. The narrow border is decorated with wild rose, daisies and grapes on a dark-blue ground.

The blue-green and reddish-brown colours have hardly faded.

Literature: *K. S. Butler:* pp. 92—104; *N. Y. Biryukova:* pp. 20—3.

67

MEDEA BEARING GIFTS TO CREON (Detail)

Medea presents the casket of poisoned gifts to Creon, who is shown as an old man with a full beard and a turban.

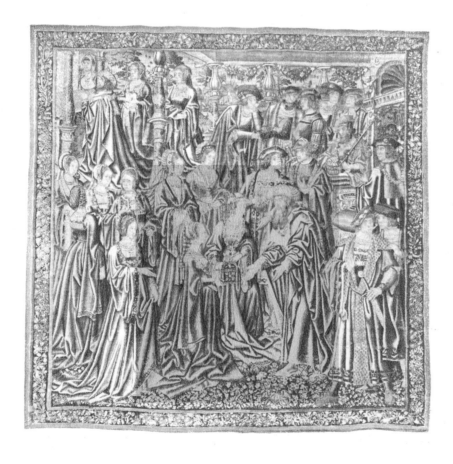

Medea bearing gifts to creon (Detail)

Meticulous attention to detail is a feature of Brussels tapestry. Medea's jewel-studded casket is typical.

Medea Bearing Gifts to Creon (Detail)

Ladies among the courtiers. The grace and dignity of these well-modelled figures exemplify the charm with which early sixteenth-century Flemish tapestry artists endowed their female subjects.

70

Medea Bearing Gifts to Creon (Detail of a young man)

The figure of the young man in a hat is interesting both for its distinctive features and for the general portrayal of emotion.

Medea bearing gifts to Creon (Detail)

The tapestry is rather worn in places, and some of the faces are damaged. However, this does not prevent an appreciation of the fine interpretation of individual characters and the masterly technique.

THE BRIDEGROOM'S PORTRAIT, from a series illustrating a mediaeval romance

Flanders, Brussels.
Early 16th century.
Wool and silk.
6—7 warp and 10—12 weft threads per cm.
2.72 × 3.32 metres.
No. T—2975.
Acquired by the Hermitage from the Stieglitz Museum in 1923.

Wearing an ermine-lined mantle and holding a sceptre, the queen sits on a throne beneath a decorated canopy. Her courtiers stand around her. A woman kneels at the queen's feet, showing her the portrait of the royal betrothed. Cupid, dressed as a young page, draws his bow, ready to strike the queen's heart with an arrow. One of the ladies-in-waiting is holding a pomegranate, the symbol of fertility, and in the foreground is a dog, the symbol of faithfulness.

The border is decorated with a ribbon of interlacing flowers — wild roses, pansies, daisies, irises and poppies — on a blue ground.

Literature: A similar tapestry called *The Betrothal* is referred to in *Collection de Somzée, 1910:* p. 73, No. 529, pl. XXII.

73

THE BRIDEGROOM'S PORTRAIT (Detail)

Courtiers surrounding the queen.

This tapestry is distinguished by the unusual treatment of the faces and especially the shape of the half-closed eyes. It is closer in type to a tapestry of a betrothal from the former Somzée collection which also appears to have been taken from a mediaeval romance (referred to in the literature for plate 73).

The restrained blue-greens and reds of the design have darkened with time. Despite their limited colour scheme the artists and weavers of Brussels achieved highly decorative effects.

THE WEDDING OF BEATRICE, from the series THE STORY OF THE SWAN KNIGHT

Flanders, Brussels.
Early 16th century.
Wool, silk, gold and silver thread.
6—8 warp and 17—18 weft threads per cm.
4.25×5.40 metres.
No. T—15619.
Acquired from the Stieglitz Museum in 1923, for which it was purchased in 1900. Formerly in the collection of Sir Richard Wallace.

The mediaeval legend *The Story of the Swan Knight* which this tapestry illustrates is the French version of *Lohengrin*. The story is summarised on pages 27—8 in the Introduction.

It is not known how many tapestries made up the original set.

In the Hermitage tapestry the bishop is seen joining the hands of King Oriens and Beatrice, under a baldaquin. Courtiers are grouped round the bridal pair. In the upper part, musicians and onlookers fill a balcony hung with cloth patterned with pomegranate and other designs. On the baldaquin is the inscription: *Rex Oriens ob amorem Beatricem ducit in uxorem.*

The border is made up of thickly worked bunches of grapes, branches of wild roses, daisies, poppies and various fruits.

Literature: *Guiffrey, Münz and Pinchard:* pl. 8; *A. Carbonier:* p. 10, No. 750; *E. H. Westfalen:* p. 16; *Ermitazh 1956:* p. 16; *K. S. Butler:* pp. 92—103, fig. 6.

75

THE WEDDING OF BEATRICE (Details)

In addition to their decorative qualities and despite the formal, hieratic composition, the sets of tapestries woven in Brussels at the beginning of the sixteenth century faithfully reflect the court life of the day. There are intriguing details of contemporary customs, festivals and ceremonies.

The *Swan Knight* tapestry is typical of this. From the balcony a lady and gentleman watch the marriage ceremony below attentively. The long, slit sleeves of the man's fur-trimmed mantle fall on the ornamental Sicilian fabric that drapes the balustrade. The couple is separated from the group of court musicians by a mosaic column.

76

77

THE WEDDING OF BEATRICE (Detail)

The name of the artist who drew the cartoon is not known, though from the style, the work is thought to be that of Jan van Room. But whoever he may have been, his great artistic abilities are shown by the remarkable expressiveness of the figures and especially their faces.

The portrayal of King Oriens resembles the work of the great graphic artists of the sixteenth century.

THE WEDDING OF BEATRICE (Detail of King Oriens)

The art of the painter who made the original sketch and of the artist who drew the cartoon is completed by the work of the weaver. The final result is his interpretation of the design in the medium of tapestry, depending on the weaver's skill, artistry and feeling for colour.

THE WEDDING OF BEATRICE (Detail)

The bishop's cope has a border of saints, which may be compared with surviving vestments of the period.

Brussels tapestry of the early sixteenth century provides a pictorial encyclopedia of courtly and ecclesiastical fashions of the time.

THE WEDDING OF BEATRICE (Detail)

In the *Swan Knight* tapestry, the Flemish artist's charming portrait of Beatrice has much in common with the character of the tender Elsa von Brabant, her German counterpart in *Lohengrin*.

THE WEDDING OF BEATRICE (Detail)

Courtiers of the king's entourage. Each person in the procession of characters reacts to the proceedings in a most lifelike way. Despite the large number of figures, no two are alike.

THE WEDDING OF BEATRICE (Detail)

Ladies and gentlemen in attendance on Beatrice.

THE WEDDING OF BEATRICE (Detail)

Among Beatrice's attendants is a man in a flat hat and a fur-trimmed grown. His dark, lively face is in sharp contrast to the portraits of the dignified ladies of the court.

THE WEDDING OF BEATRICE (Detail)

This portrait is outstanding. It is a young girl among the ladies-in-waiting, looking into the distance with a tender, dreamy expression. This poetic portrayal has much in common with the appealing heroines of mediaeval romances.

THE WEDDING OF BEATRICE (Detail)

Ladies-in-waiting.

THE WEDDING OF BEATRICE (Detail)

In the foreground of this tapestry is a lively incident, with no obvious connection with the main subject.

A young man in rich court garments has taken off his hat to bow and present a book to a lady who is half turned towards him.

THE WEDDING OF BEATRICE (Detail)

The pomegranate pattern of the drapery hanging over the balcony resembles the design often found on fifteenth-century Italian brocade.

THE TRIUMPH OF BEATRICE, from the series THE STORY OF THE SWAN KNIGHT

Flanders, Brussels.
Early 16th century.
Wool, silk, gold and silver threads.
6—8 warp and 17—20 weft threads per cm.
4.23 × 5.38 metres.
No. T—15618.
Acquired from the Stieglitz Museum in 1923, for which it had been purchased in 1900.
Formerly in the collection of Sir Richard Wallace.

The tapestry shows Beatrice returning to the palace in a carriage drawn by white horses. She is dressed in a brilliant fur-trimmed mantle, and is accompanied by a ceremonial procession of courtiers. Numerous onlookers are crowded on balconies draped with decorative hangings.

   Literature: *E. Münz:* p. 156; *A. Carbonier:* p. 40, No. 749; *E. H. Westfalen:* p. 16; *Ermitazh, 1956:* pp. 15, 16; *K. S. Butler:* pp. 92—103, fig. 6.

89

THE TRIUMPH OF BEATRICE (Details)

The townspeople have crowded to the draped and decorated balconies of their homes to welcome Beatrice.

The architectural background is a combination of Gothic and Renaissance elements. We notice Gothic tracery alongside pillars with typical Renaissance grotesques.

90

91

THE TRIUMPH OF BEATRICE (Detail)

Men and boys with flaming torches accompany the festive procession. Each detail records customs of the times.

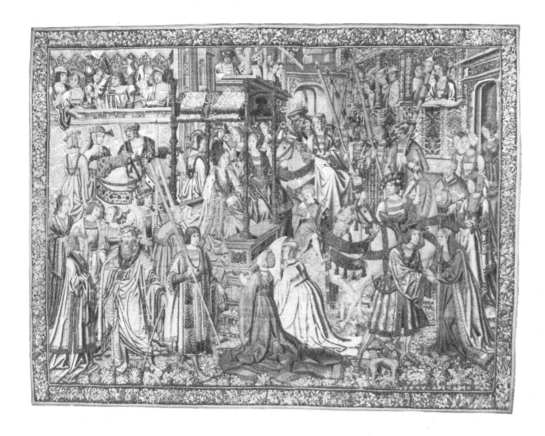

THE TRIUMPH OF BEATRICE (Detail)

Above the crowd, through a stone arch decorated with tracery, we can see the sky and the spire of a Gothic church against it.

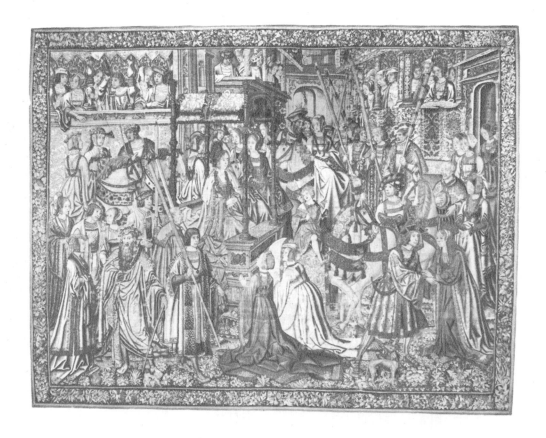

THE TRIUMPH OF BEATRICE (Detail)

All the costumes and head-dresses shown in the *Swan Knight* tapestries closely resemble those in the contemporary engravings and drawings of these subjects (*Trachtenstudien*) by Holbein and Dürer.

94

THE TRIUMPH OF BEATRICE (Detail)

In the foreground is the figure of a majestic, bearded old man and a slender youth in a fur-trimmed gown. These are among the most typical of all the figures that fill the sixteenth-century Brussels tapestries. Whatever the subject, similar types of people in similar costumes are found on many tapestries. This is due to the close links existing between the different workshops, to the sharing of cartoons, and to the fact that the same artists were employed by different masters. At the same time, the weavers often altered the cartoons themselves: for example, when they needed special dimensions for a given tapestry. They would take one or two figures from other cartoons to fill in odd space, or to use the new shape better.

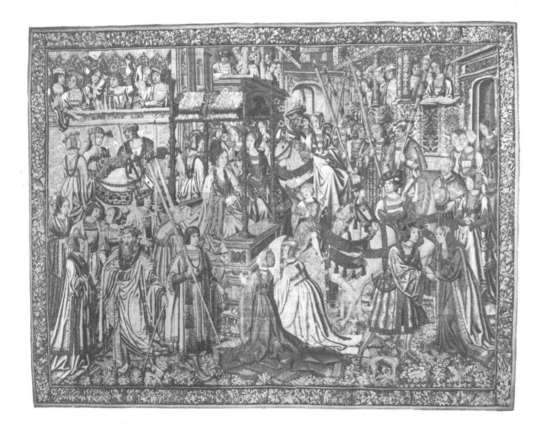

THE TRIUMPH OF BEATRICE (Detail)

Young man in a fur-trimmed gown.

THE TRIUMPH OF BEATRICE (Detail)

Beatrice wears an ermine-trimmed mantle sewn with precious stones and a high wimple.

The tapestry is richly woven with gold and silver threads which are now rather tarnished. They only gleam when a strong light is thrown on them, but then the gold and silver sparkles again luxuriantly, for a moment bringing back its original splendour.

THE TRIUMPH OF BEATRICE (Detail)

A comparison between the tender and poetic Beatrice of the *Wedding* tapestry and the sorrowful woman of the *Triumph* tapestry shows a considerable evolution of character.

At the beginning of the sixteenth century, the cartoon artists and weavers, while maintaining the decorative qualities of the composition, gave much more significance to the logical unfolding of events than was the case in the preceding century.

THE TRIUMPH OF BEATRICE (Detail)

The great spreading folds of the long gowns worn by kneeling women are a favourite motif in mediaeval tapestry, where the greatest use was made of them for decorative effect. The treatment of drapery is extraordinarily successful in the *Swan Knight* series. Here the broken Gothic folds, which still to a certain extent maintain the old style, flow much more softly.

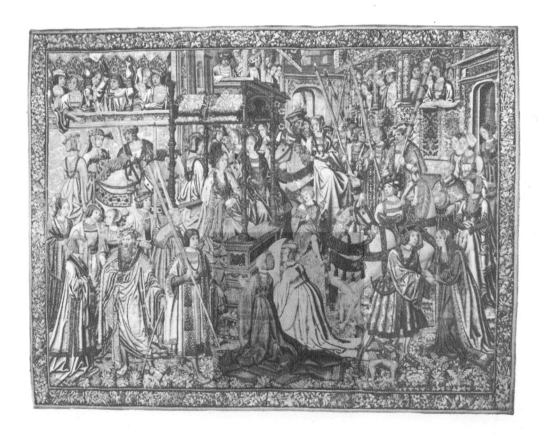

THE TRIUMPH OF BEATRICE (Detail)

The somewhat conventional white horse, with its fancifully designed and bejewelled harness, follows the tradition of the medium where the composition is treated not as a painting or even as a mural, but as a decorative hanging.

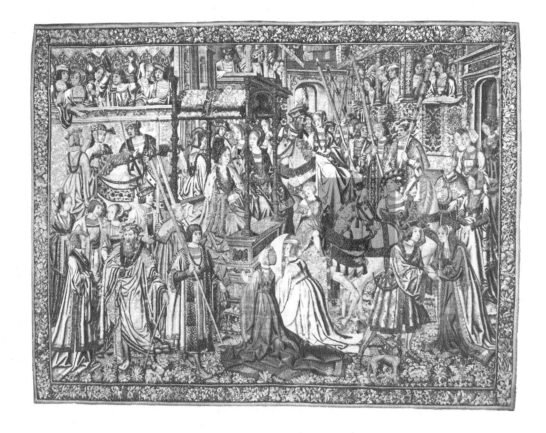

THE TRIUMPH OF BEATRICE (Detail)

The dull shimmer of the gold and silver particularly enhances the colour harmony of yellows and blues.

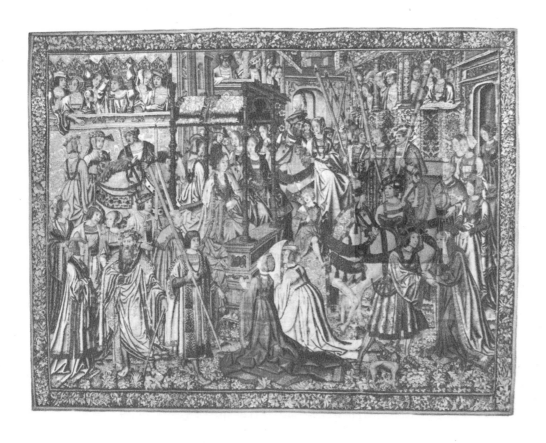

THE TRIUMPH OF BEATRICE (Detail)

A detail showing the subtle use of shading to achieve the modelling of a face and the texture of hair and material.

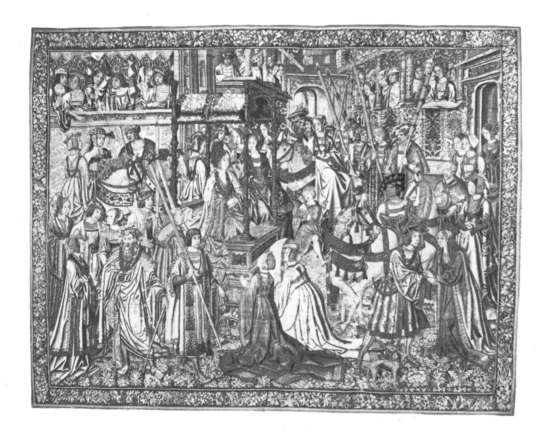

THE TRIUMPH OF BEATRICE (Detail)

At first, these lovers stepping towards each other seem to have no connection with the story. But the importance of the figures, the rich costumes studded with precious stones, woven from gold and silver thread, and above all, the lady's crown, prove them to be Oriens and Beatrice reunited.

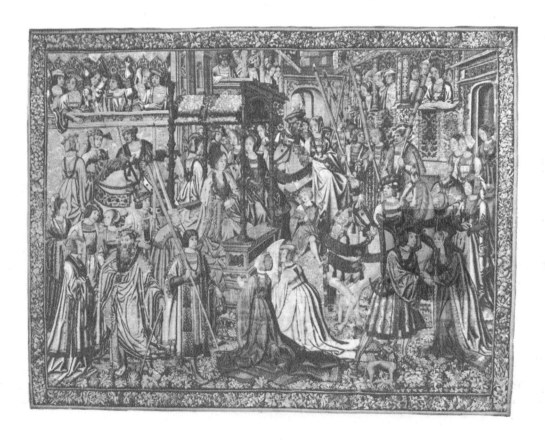

THE TRIUMPH OF BEATRICE (Detail)

The finely drawn sprays of flowers are an important part of early Brussels tapestry. Though stylised with great taste and feeling for the medium, they nevertheless keep their distinctive forms as flowers.

They fill all the free space, making for unity between the different elements of composition, and giving each tapestry a decorative quality peculiar to the classic period of tapestry weaving.

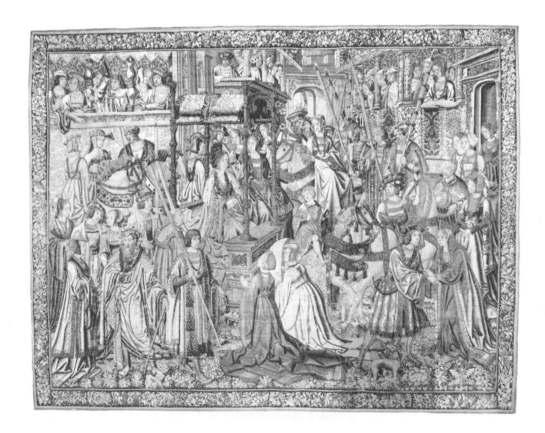

104

THE TRIUMPH OF BEATRICE (Details)

The decorative border is an integral part of early sixteenth-century Flemish tapestry. Most borders of this period are made up of intertwining garlands of wild roses, daisies or grapes.

These borders were used in Brussels, but the flat, conventional manner of designing the flowers, gradually gave way to a freer and more vivid form. The borders of the *Swan Knight* tapestries contain a variety of flowers and fruit, perfectly drawn and woven with great skill.

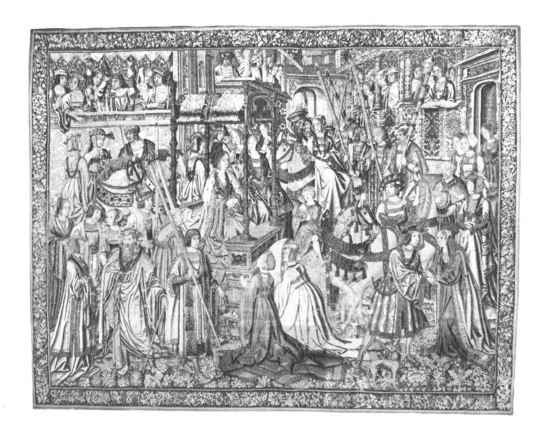

105

106

BOUCHE D'OR BECOMES THE VASSAL OF AMOUR, from the series THE ROMAUNT OF THE ROSE

Flanders, Brussels.
Early 16th century.
Wool, silk, gold and silver threads.
6—8 warp and 14—16 weft threads per cm.
4.25 × 4.07 metres.
No. T—2925.
Acquired from the Stieglitz Museum in 1923, for which it had been purchased in 1900. Formerly in the collection of Sir Richard Wallace.

The romance known as *The Romaunt of the Rose* is the work of two authors. It was begun in the first half of the thirteenth century by Guillaume de Lorris, and finished at the end of the century by Jean de Meung. Written in the form of an allegorical dream, it tells of a young man's love for the Rose. In the Hermitage tapestry set narrating the tale, he is called *Bouche d'Or*.

Several episodes are shown on each tapestry, but the development of the story is very fragmentary and differs considerably from the original poem. The total number of pieces in the series is not known.

In the upper part of the tapestry called *Bouche d'Or Becomes the Vassal of Amour*, the young man is kneeling before the throne of Amour to swear his fidelity. Around him are the inhabitants of the enchanted garden, the trusted friends and helpers of the God of Love, interpreted as beautiful women. Many of these figures have names woven round them, such as *Bel acceil* (Welcome), *Doul[c]e parler* (Sweet Speech), and *Doul[c]e regard* (Sweet Glance).

On the lower part of the tapestry, Bouche d'Or stands before a warrior in a winged helmet called *Male bouche* (Bitter Tongue). The artist has also drawn Male bouche's allies, *Traison* (Treason) and *Despit* (Spite) who have shut Bouche d'Or's friend, the young man *Accueil*, in the Castle of Jealousy. Beside Male bouche, the artist has drawn *Faux semblant* (Hypocrisy), dressed as a friar, although this character only figures in the second part of the *Romaunt* — as an ally of the God of Love. Beyond the fence, bearing a cudgel, stands the Rose's faithful guard, *Dangier* (Danger).

In the foreground, the female figure personifying Nature kneels at an anvil. On the flagged floor of the upper scene are the letters R.S.L.A. One flagstone, in the centre of the tapestry, bears a bold letter A.

The narrow border is made up of grapes and roses.

Literature: *Guiffrey, Müntz and Pinchart:* plate 10; *A. Carbonier:* p. 40, No. 752; *H. Göbel, I, 1923:* pp. 77—9; *E. H. Westfalen:* p. 16; *Ermitazh, 1956:* pp. 14—15.

107

BOUCHE D'OR BECOMES THE VASSAL OF AMOUR (Details)

Judging by the perfection of the work and the fine elaboration of detail, the *Romaunt of the Rose* set was woven in one of the best Brussels workshops.

The composition is like that of most sixteenth-century tapestries, but the treatment of the figures, of certain landscape details and of the architectural background has a good deal in common stylistically with the work of the most famous of all the cartoon artists, Bernard van Orley, whose name is coupled with the beginning of a new style in Flemish tapestry.

108

109

Bouche d'Or Becomes the Vassal of Amour (Detail)

The Romaunt of the Rose, particularly the first part, is a poem of love written in the decorous and refined language of chivalry. The poem begins with the words:

> Ci est le Roman de la Rose
> Ou l'art d'amour est tout enclose.

> Here is the story of the Rose
> Wherein the art of love is all contained.

The centre of this tapestry is taken up by the God of Love, one of the main characters in the romance. There is a good deal of symbolism attached to his portrait, which shows him as a winged youth. His rich gown, embroidered with the pomegranate motif, is regally trimmed with ermine. His eyes are bound with a flimsy veil.

Bouche d'or becomes the vassal of Amour (Details)

The woven inscriptions give the names of many of the characters in this tapestry. The woman clothed in mail, who bears in one hand a buckler and in the other a violet-strewn banner, is *Pruderie* (Modesty). The young girl with a bunch of wild flowers is *Doul[c]e regard*. *Folie* (Madness) wears a ridiculous and extravagant head-dress. Not all the figures have these woven inscriptions; but even so, it is not difficult to guess who are Love's allies and who his enemies. It is clear from the way the different people are portrayed and from the accessories they bear.

III

II2

BOUCHE D'OR BECOMES THE VASSAL OF AMOUR (Detail)

There is no proper sequence to the episodes shown on the tapestry. We can find, side by side, the characters described by Guillaume de Lorris in the first part of the romance, and those of Jean de Meung in the second part.

Nature is one of the main characters in the second part, and Jean de Meung, a cultivated man remarkable for his freedom of thought, wrote bold speeches for her. It is thanks to Nature's intervention that the tale comes to a happy end.

In the following lines from the *Romaunt*, the poet describes Nature as a woman who, toiling in her smithy, labours for the propagation of mankind:

> Comment Nature la subtille
> Forge toujours ou fils ou fille,
> Afin que l'humaine ligne
> Par son defaut ne faillmye.
>
> How clever Nature is
> ever forging either a son or a daughter,
> in order that the human line
> should not fail by any fault of hers.

THE BATTLE, from the series THE ROMAUNT OF THE ROSE

Flanders, Brussels.
Early 16th century.
Wool, silk, gold and silver threads.
6—8 warp and 14—16 weft threads per cm.
4.25×4.07 metres.
No. T—2924.
Acquired from the Stieglitz Museum in 1923, for which it had been purchased in 1900. Formerly in the collection of Sir Richard Wallace.

This tapestry depicts a battle between the God of Love's friends and enemies. Amour's friends, the allies of the Rose's lover, Bouche d'Or, are *Perseverance*, *Largesse*, *Courtoisie*,

Plaisance, *Espoir* and *Franchise*. They are beautiful women, holding bunches of flowers. Their enemies are *Male bouche*, *Traison*, *Vilonie*, *Despit* and *Faulte Deseus*.

In the upper middle scene, a young man on a throne is being crowned with flowers by two girls, *Obediance* and *Dignité*. This is probably Bouche d'Or's friend *Acceuil*, who has been set free from the Castle of Jealousy.

The narrow border is made up of grapes, wild roses and daisies.

Literature: *Guiffrey, Münz and Pinchart:* plate 9; *A. Carbonier:* p. 40, No. 751; *H. Göbel, I, 1923:* pp. 77—9; *E. H. Westfalen:* p. 16; *Ermitazh, 1956:* pp. 14, 15.

114

THE BATTLE (Detail)

Franchise is dressed as a huntress, shooting roses from a cross-bow. *Courtoisie*'s weapon is a spray of tiny flowers, and *Plaisance* is armed with a bunch of enormous pansies. These three are in the centre of the composition.

THE BATTLE (Detail)

Largesse and *Espoir*, armed with flowers.

Group of Men and Women with an Oak Tree (Fragment)

Flanders, Brussels.
Early 16th century.
Wool and silk.
6—7 warp and 14—16 weft threads per cm.
1.34×1.01 metres.
No. T—6913.
Acquired from the Stieglitz Museum in 1923. Purchased in Vienna in 1886.

Two men and two women in rich costumes are shown against the background of an oak tree.

Because the lower part of the figures is missing, and a landscape spreads out above them, this fragment is clearly a section cut from the upper part of a tapestry. A border has been sewn along the bottom edge, composed of sprays of wild roses, pea pods and pomegranates, their stems closely intertwined.

Greens and reds predominate.

Group of Men and Women with an Oak Tree (Detail)

117

118

THE APPARITION OF THE VIRGIN MARY, from the series THE LEGEND OF OUR LADY OF THE SABLON

Flanders, Brussels.
1518—1519.
The cartoon may have been designed by Bernard van Orley.
Wool and silk.
6—7 warp and 16—18 weft threads per cm.
3.45 × 5.43 metres.
No. T—2976.

The cartoons for this series of tapestries were ordered in 1518 by François Thurn de Taxis, the master of the imperial post. Only one set was made. Until the end of the eighteenth century the four pieces were hung in the church of Notre-Dame du Sablon, in Brussels. Then, having passed through several hands, they came into the collection of F. Spitzer, who cut the first and third tapestries each into three parts. In 1893 all the tapestries (the two complete works and the two cut-up ones) were sold. The second tapestry was purchased through the antique dealer Lowengard for the Stieglitz Museum, and from there it came to the Hermitage in 1923. The fragments of the tapestries which were cut up were for many years in the collections of Sir William Burrell and Lord Astor of Hever. The tapestries from the Astor collection were sold in 1963 and returned to Brussels, to the Musées Royaux d'Art et d'Histoire, Parc du Cinquante-naire.

The tapestries tell the story of the statue of the Virgin in Notre-Dame du Sablon, Brussels. The Virgin Mary appeared to the pious Beatrice of Antwerp, and told her to take the statue of the Madonna from the cathedral at Antwerp to be restored and regilded. When Beatrice had done this, the Virgin Mary again appeared to her and told her to take the statue to the Brussels church. But the sacristan of Antwerp Cathedral refused to let her do so. For the third time, the Virgin Mary appeared to Beatrice and insisted that she should carry out her bidding. So Beatrice took the statue from the cathedral and put it on a ship bound for Brussels. There the Duke of Brabant, accompanied by his court, came to meet the ship and, with much ceremony, the statue was borne through the streets to the church of Notre-Dame du Sablon.

All the tapestries of this set are divided into three parts by slim columns, each part relating a different episode. The Hermitage tapestry is the second of the series. The left-hand panel shows the Virgin Mary surrounded by angels, appearing to Beatrice in the second vision, and telling her to take the statue from Antwerp to Brussels.

The middle panel shows the altar of Antwerp Cathedral before which stand four important burghers and the sacristan. Beatrice is begging them to let her take the statue, but they refuse.

The right-hand panel shows the third apparition of the Virgin, who repeats her request.

The columns that divide the tapestry are crowned with angels bearing the arms of the houses of Aragon, Castile and León and the house of Aragon and Sicily.

The border is composed of arabesques and scrolls of an explanatory Latin text, woven against a red background.

The great ornamental letters at the beginning of each scroll indicate the order in which the lines should be read:

119

F   Illa quiescebat rursus sub nocte silenti
     Delabi superis visa Maria polis

G Effatur: nostram referas ex aede figuram
     Hac Sabulina decet preside templa frui.

H Hec sacrata movet properos ad limina gressus
     Sed negat optatam dura repulsa deam.

I   Nox ruit et vultu dive redeuntis eodem
     Forma soporanti talia visa loqui:

K Eia age pone metum statuam volo sub lege nostra
     Ipsa ego presenti patroscinabor ope.

F   The old woman rested again in the silence of the night. Mary, seeming to come down from above,

G Says: Bring back our image from the church. It is fitting that the sanctuaries of Sablon should rejoice in the protection of my image.

H The woman hastens towards the holy place, but is harshly refused the Madonna she desires.

I   Night falls, and the vision of the Virgin, returning with the same expression, seems to say to the drowsing woman the following words:

K Come, fear not, I wish the statue to be under our law, I myself shall protect you.

In the middle of the upper border are the arms of the Holy Roman Empire, flanked on each side by a cornucopia.

The border on the left side contains the arms of Thurn de Taxis in a shield with a wild boar and eaglets. Above and below it run curling scrolls with the motto: *Habeo quod dedi*. The right-hand shield displays lions and the motto: *Dum vixit bene, bene vixit*, the arms of Thurn de Taxis's mother.

Literature: *E. Müntz:* p. 196; *Collection Spitzer:* pp. 158—61, 165—8, plate VII; *Destrée and van den Ven:* p. 28, plates 25—7; *H. Göbel, I, 1923:* pp. 138, 141, 441; *M. Crick-Kuntziger:* pp. 1—4; *Ermitazh, 1956:* p. 16; *W. Wells:* pp. 7—10, 29; *R. A. d'Hulst:* pp. 139—44.

THE APPARITION OF THE VIRGIN MARY (Detail)

Beatrice is shown on a couch with a rich covering draped in broken folds. The figure is boldly foreshortened so that the rich folds of the cloth stand out. The sensitive face and hands indicate a talented designer and a skilled weaver.

THE APPARITION OF THE VIRGIN MARY (Detail)

The Virgin bids Beatrice to take her statue from Antwerp to Brussels.

Mary bears the Child in her arms and is surrounded by angels, a traditional manner of representing her.

THE APPARITION OF THE VIRGIN MARY (Detail)

From the excellence of the portraits, the quality of the design and the fact that many members of the house of Habsburg are depicted in the tapestry, we can conclude that the set was designed by Bernard van Orley, court artist to Margaret of Austria, the regent of the Netherlands.

THE APPARITION OF THE VIRGIN MARY (Detail)

The detail shows the subtle use of dovetailed colours of different shades to achieve both texture and modelling. Compare with plate 102.

THE APPARITION OF THE VIRGIN MARY (Detail)

The sacristan refuses to let Beatrice take away the statue of the Virgin.

This may well be the portrait of a real person. Thurn de Taxis himself is frequently shown among the members of the house of Habsburg, who come to receive the statue when the ship docks. So are de Taxis's wife and nephew, as well as other historical figures of the day. For example, on the third tapestry there is a figure which is either Loredano, Doge of Venice, or his envoy, while on the fourth we can find Philibert of Savoy, husband of Margaret of Austria.

THE APPARITION OF THE VIRGIN MARY (Detail)

The pious Beatrice begs to be allowed to take the statue. The legend had it that she came from a modest family and was herself a humble spinner. This is how the artist imagined her, repeating the same figure in the many episodes of the series.

THE APPARITION OF THE VIRGIN MARY (Details)

The altar of Antwerp Cathedral.

In the Sablon series the figures do not occupy the whole surface of the tapestry. They are few in number and are disposed in the foreground.

The middle distance is used to express space and here we see an attempt to show an interior perspective.

126

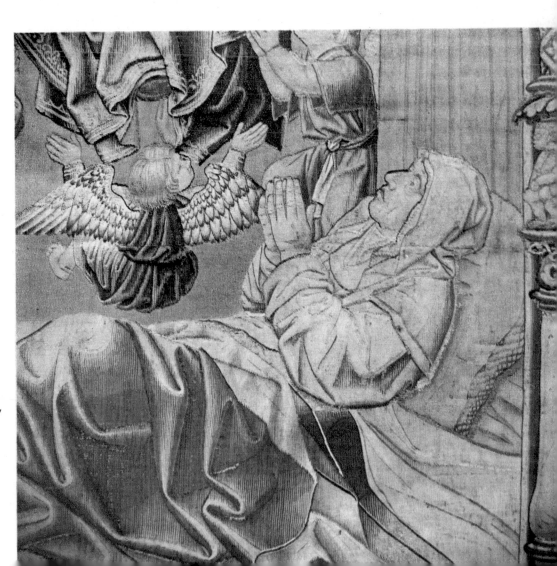

127

THE APPARITION OF THE VIRGIN MARY (Detail)

A guttering candle in a homely candlestick stands on a small bench with fine panelled carving, and on the floor are Beatrice's clogs. These small but valuable details illustrate the everyday life of the people at the time when these tapestries were woven.

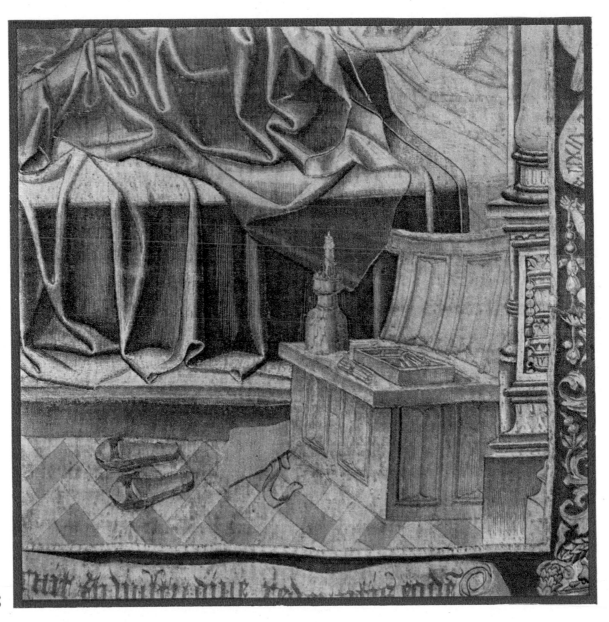